Mark Twain and Little Satan

Title: Mark Twain and Little Satan

The Writing of

The Mysterious Stranger

by
John S. Tuckey

1963
West Lafayette
PURDUE UNIVERSITY STUDIES

For Irene, Janis, and Alan

ACKNOWLEDGMENTS

I am grateful to Henry Nash Smith, literary editor of the Mark Twain Papers, and to Frederick Anderson, librarian of the Papers, for their kind and indispensable help on many occasions; to Walter Blair, University of Chicago, who has read an early draft of the manuscript; to Ray Browne, Richard Combs, Carl H. Elliott, Paul Fatout, Robin Friedheim, William Gass, Walter Hartmann, Charles H. Lawshe, Barriss Mills, Robert Ogle, Lucille Schendera, William Stafford, and Sigrid Stark, Purdue University, for much assistance and counsel. I remain grateful to John T. Frederick and Ernest E. Sandeen, University of Notre Dame, under whose guidance I first undertook the study of Mark Twain's writings some fourteen years ago. For grants which made possible my study of Mark Twain materials at the General Library of the University of California, Berkeley, and at the Huntington Library, I am grateful to the Purdue Research Foundation. And to the University of California Press my especial thanks are due for permission to quote from hitherto unpublished Mark Twain materials. For permission to quote from books and articles, I make grateful acknowledgment to the following: To Harper & Brothers for excerpts from *Following the Equator* and *The Mysterious Stranger,* by Mark Twain; from *Mark Twain: A Biography, Mark Twain's Letters,* and *Mark Twain's Notebook,* all edited by Albert Bigelow Paine. To Harper & Row for excerpts from Mark Twain, *Letters From the Earth,* edited by Bernard DeVoto. To Harvard University Press for excerpts from Bernard DeVoto, *Mark Twain at Work,* and *Mark Twain-Howells Letters,* edited by Henry Nash Smith and William Gibson with the assistance of Frederick Anderson. To the *Mark Twain Journal,* edited by Cyril Clemens, for excerpts from Max Lederer, "Mark Twain in Vienna," *Mark Twain Quarterly.* To Charles Neider, editor of *Mark Twain: Life As I Find It.* To Doris Webster, wife of the late Samuel Charles Webster, author of *Mark Twain, Business Man.*

J. S. T.

January, 1963

1

THE MYSTERIOUS STRANGER has become recognized as the most important of Mark Twain's later writings. Two decades have passed since Bernard DeVoto, having studied the unpublished drafts of the tale and also many related manuscripts, termed the work a highly "important key to Mark Twain's books" and announced that he hoped some day to tell the story of Mark Twain's writing of *The Mysterious Stranger*. He was planning such a book-length study—one that would throw some light "into many areas of Mark Twain's personality that have so far been dark." But he did not live to write such a book and to share with his readers the fascination of "working on a mystery story" and discovering clues to "the unconscious workings" of the author's mind.[1] Although *The Mysterious Stranger* has in recent years received much critical attention,[2] the times and circumstances of its composition have nevertheless remained largely unknown.

The story exists in three quite different drafts, all in Twain's own handwriting, which were left unfinished when he died in 1910. These are, as named and catalogued by DeVoto, the "Hannibal" manuscript of about 15,300 words; the "Eseldorf" of 55,000 words; and the "Print Shop" of 65,000 words.[3] All of these manuscripts are in the Mark Twain Papers, which are stored at the General Library of the University of California, Berkeley. There has been much uncertainty concerning the direction and tendency of the creative efforts that produced these several drafts; in particular, it has remained doubtful whether the posthumously published tale represents the initial, the intermediate, or the latest version.

Six years after Mark Twain's death, *The Mysterious Stranger* was published as edited by Albert Bigelow Paine, the author's biographer and literary executor, and Frederick A. Duneka, then general manager of Harper & Brothers.[4] For the text, the editors used the "Eseldorf" version, completing the story with a chapter that Paine had found, separate from any of the versions, among the many manuscripts and fragments in the Papers. The setting for the story is the village of Eseldorf, in Austria; the time is 1590, "still the Middle Ages" in a remote and sleep-rounded region. Twain's naive narrator, young Theodor Fischer, explains, "Austria was far from the world, and asleep, and our village was in the middle of that sleep, being in the middle of Austria. It drowsed in peace in the deep privacy of a hilly and woodsy solitude where news from the world hardly ever came to disturb its dreams, and was infinitely content." The place "was a paradise for us boys. We were not overmuch pestered with schooling."[5] But Theodor is destined to discover that Eseldorf (i.e., Ass-ville) is only a fool's paradise. Into the deceptively idyllic setting comes a mysterious stranger, appearing to Theodor and his friends Nikolaus Bauman and Seppi Wohlmeyer as a young angel, unfallen but nephew to the fallen Satan, and bearing the same name. The young Satan has unlimited powers of mind. He discloses that he knows the entire chain of future consequences that will result from any action.[6] He is also able to read anyone's thoughts. Moreover, his thoughts are equivalent to actions; he has, for example, but to think of a journey and it is at once accomplished.[7] Even this power is not the most wonderful of his abilities. "My mind creates," he tells the startled youngsters. "Do you get the force of that? . . . Creates fluids, solids, colors—anything, everything—out of the airy nothing which is called Thought."[8] Before the eyes of his astonished comrades, he makes a group of tiny people, who promptly go to work and build a miniature castle; thereafter, he sets the castle on fire and, when the little people run out, brushes them back into the flames, saying that "they were of no value."[9] And it soon becomes apparent that he regards all men as equally worthless.

Sitting in judgment upon the human race, Satan finds it contemptible: "Man's limited mind clumsily and tediously and laboriously patches little trivialities together"—for a paltry result.[10] Also, the Moral Sense has corrupted man: knowing good and evil, he has the opportunity to choose to do evil.[11] And, besides being mentally and morally of no value, man is physically of negligible worth, "a museum of disease, a home of impurities; he comes to-day and is gone tomorrow; he begins as dirt and departs as stench."[12] Satan takes the boys on instantaneous journeys about the globe, exhibiting to them the frailties and depravities of their species. So wretched is the human condition that, by his calculation, not one life in a billion is worth living; he can do a person no greater kindness than granting him an early death.[13] However, he does have one way of making people happy while they are in life. When Father Peter, the good priest of the village, is falsely accused of theft, tried, and acquitted, Satan makes him believe that he has been "forever disgraced as a thief—by verdict of the court!" The old man's reason is unseated by the shock of this false news; he becomes insane, fancies himself the Emperor of Austria, and is "the one utterly happy person in this empire." When the boys of Eseldorf regret that this contentment has been purchased at such a cost, the mysterious stranger admonishes them, "Are you so unobservant as not to have found out that sanity and happiness are an impossible combination? No sane man can be happy, for to him life is real, and he sees what a fearful thing it is."[14] Illusion is shown to be man's only refuge. Finally, in the closing chapter—the one found and added by Paine—Satan reveals that illusion is, indeed, the basis of existence: *"Life itself is only a vision, a dream."* He tells the narrator, "I am but a dream—your dream, creature of your imagination. In a moment you will have realized this, then you will banish me from your visions and I shall dissolve into the nothingness out of which you made me." And Satan vanishes, after this valediction: "It is true, that which I have revealed to you; there is no God, no universe, no human race, no earthly life, no heaven, no hell. It is all a dream—a grotesque and foolish dream. Nothing exists but you. And you are but a *thought*—a vagrant thought, a useless thought, a homeless thought, wandering forlorn among the empty eternities!"[15]

DeVoto thought that Mark Twain had, in writing the "Eseldorf" version and the "dream ending," arrived at a saving solution of an overwhelming personal problem. He believed that a series of misfortunes—financial reverses, loss of health, the death of his daughter Susy, and the discovery that another daughter, Jean, was an epileptic—had induced a sense of failure and guilt; had impaired Twain's "secret image of himself" and withered his talent. For a period of seven or eight years, he found, the despairing author had tried desperately to regain his creative abilities but had found his "compulsive need to write . . . constantly blocked, displaced, and distorted." He considered the period of lowest ebb of Twain's literary talent to be "the two and a half years following . . . May 18, 1897," when his prose had become "dead" in a "time of impotence and failure."[16] And he believed that "Eseldorf" had been written about 1905,[17] as the latest version of *The Mysterious Stranger* and as the final outcome of Twain's many earlier attempts to create in terms of his "symbols of despair": it was the work "that came through to triumph at the last . . . to achieve the completion denied its many predecessors, the book which we know as *The Mysterious Stranger*." By writing it, DeVoto theorized, Twain had "saved himself in the end" and had come "back from the edge of insanity." "The dream" had been "the answer and the proof":

> Or, if I may so phrase it, we see the psychic block removed, the dilemma solved, the inhibition broken, the accusation stilled, and Mark Twain's mind given peace at last and his talent restored. The miracles, which at first are just an idle game for the amusement of the boys and the astonishment of the villagers, become finally a spectacle of human life in miniature, with the suffering diminished to the vanishing point since these are just puppets, unreal creatures moving in a shadow-play, and they are seen with the detachment of an immortal spirit, passionless and untouched. And so from a spectacle they become a dream—the symbolic dream of human experience that Mark had been trying to write in such travail for so many years.[18]

The thesis of DeVoto as here stated has gained very general acceptance and has been used as a basis for explaining what happened to Mark Twain and to his work during his later years. Nevertheless, the conclusions that have been drawn rest upon assumptions about an unknown chronology. DeVoto attempted to follow Twain's themes "rather by idea than by manuscript," acknowledging, "I cannot be sure that my arrangement is chronological."[19] However, he did perforce make assumptions regarding the times of composition of the writings that he considered, as when he stated that "the themes come together in the end,"[20] that "Eseldorf" "came through to triumph at the last,"[21] and that Twain, by writing it, "saved himself in the end."[22] It is fair to add that DeVoto stressed that he was making "a report only" concerning materials he planned to examine more fully;[23] it has already been mentioned that his death prevented his completion of such a study.

His preliminary survey had led him to suppose that, in composing the drafts of *The Mysterious Stranger*, Twain had written first the "Hannibal" version as a "fumbling and tentative" account of "marvelous works done by the young angel for the admiration and stupefaction of the village"; later the "Print Shop" version, including a shop "such as young Sam Clemens worked in," but with the scene laid in Austria during the Middle Ages; and finally the "Eseldorf" version, using again the Austrian setting but this time bringing the story to a successful completion, "after it had been painfully written over and changed and adjusted and transformed."[24] Actually, DeVoto's thesis—that Twain, after a long period of literary impotence, had restored his talent in writing "Eseldorf"—*required* the assumption that this version had been written quite late in Mark Twain's lifetime. This assumption ran counter to what Paine had recorded relative to the dating of *The Mysterious Stranger*. In discussing the writing that Twain had been doing at the beginning of 1898, much of which did not then "find its way into print," Paine mentioned in his *Biography* the existence of "three bulky manuscripts" in which the author had "attempted to set down some episodes in the life of one 'Young Satan,' a nephew, who appears to have visited among the planets and promoted some astonishing adventures in Austria several centuries ago."[25] Paine had perhaps not yet examined these materials closely (he did not undertake the editing and publication of *The Mysterious Stranger* until several years later). In only one of the existing versions—the "Eseldorf"—is Satan a nephew. Paine does not in the *Biography* attempt any specific dating of these manuscripts, but his reference to them at this point indicates his belief that Twain had worked upon a story of "Young Satan"—or, more particularly, "Eseldorf"—early in 1898. Later, in an introduction that he wrote for the Definitive Edition, Paine said flatly that *The Mysterious Stranger* "was written at Vienna, during the early part of 1898."[26] He further stated that Twain "made three extended attempts at this story, and one of them—the first, and by far the best—he brought very nearly to conclusion. Then he put these various beginnings away and did not examine them again for many years."[27] Paine also recalled that Twain had on one occasion at Stormfield (his home at Redding from June, 1908,

until his death) told him, "I always had a good deal of fancy for
that story of mine, 'The Mysterious Stranger.' I could finish it, I
suppose, any time, and I should like it some day to be published."
Then, Paine related, "a considerable time after his death—after
the publication of my biography of him . . . I found among a confusion of papers that tremendous final chapter, which must have
been written about the time of our conversation. It may even
have been written prior to that time, laid aside, and forgotten."[28]
Finally, in editing *Mark Twain's Notebook,* which was published
in 1935, Paine partly contradicted his earlier statements. He spoke
of Twain's entry regarding a "little Satan Jr. who came to Hannibal," which had been noted late in the fall of 1898, as a "hint
of the story of *The Mysterious Stranger* which he presently began
and partly finished, in three different forms."[29] This account of
the matter is, of course, incompatible with the previous assertion
that the published story, and thus "Eseldorf," had been written
in "the early part of 1898."

DeVoto readily discounted or disregarded Paine's remarks, for he
considered that Paine had not understood the significance of the
later manuscripts and had not adequately dealt with them.[30] Yet
DeVoto regarded his own conclusions as only tentative. No doubt,
had the time been given to him, he would have proved or dis-
proved his own theory that the "Eseldorf" version was the last
draft of *The Mysterious Stranger* and the work by which, after repeated literary failures, "the fallen angel of our literature, the
mysterious stranger who seemed only a sojourner in the cramped
spaces of our mortal world, saved himself in the end."[31] Since
the publication of those preliminary findings, no one has confirmed
or refuted them by determining the actual chronology of Twain's
writing of *The Mysterious Stranger* and showing the personal and
literary significance of his work upon the story.

The present book is the product of an intensive study of the
three holographic versions and of other manuscripts and fragments
written by Twain after 1895.[32] His working notes, marginalia,
notebooks, autobiographical dictations, correspondence, and published works have also been considered, as well as relevant critical
and biographical studies. The findings differ from what has here-
tofore been supposed, indicating a chronology that is substantially
the reverse of the one assumed by DeVoto. Mark Twain, it will

be seen, began "Eseldorf" not as the last but as the first of the existing versions. Indeed, he wrote the greater part of it during the two-and-one-half-year period that DeVoto believed had been most of all the "time of impotence and failure," the "time of desolation whose symbol he was not yet able to forge,"[33] and thus, according to DeVoto's theory, at a time when he should have lacked the talent to write it.

The concluding chapter will present a summary of the findings and some remarks concerning their probable significance. The other chapters will be devoted mainly to a detailed demonstration of the times and circumstances of Mark Twain's composition of the versions of *The Mysterious Stranger*. Insofar as possible, a chronological order of presentation will be followed, with the hope of affording the reader some idea of the mainstream flow of Mark Twain's creative efforts through a period of eleven years.

2

THE MYSTERIOUS STRANGER, as published, begins with a description of the sleepy village of Eseldorf, "in the middle of Austria."[34] It is possible to show that Mark Twain began his story in Austria in fact as well as in his fiction. There is evidence that he started writing it either late in 1897 or very early in 1898, and that "Eseldorf," which has been generally thought to have been written last, was begun before either "Hannibal" or "Print Shop."

After having spent the summer at Weggis, Lake Lucerne, Switzerland, Twain moved with his family to Vienna, where he took residence at the Hotel Metropole on September 28, 1897.[35] He was received with great acclaim, and his quarters at the Metropole soon resembled "a court, where with those of social rank assembled the foremost authors, journalists, diplomats, painters, philosophers, scientists, of Europe, and therefore of the world. A sister of the Emperor of Germany lived at the Metropole that winter and was especially cordial. Mark Twain's daily movements were chronicled as if he had been some visiting potentate."[36] During the early part of his stay, however, an illness kept him from taking an active part in the life of the Austrian capital. As Max Lederer has noted, Twain was suffering from what he described as a "toothache in the big toe"—presumably an attack of gout; he "received his guests in bed, clad in a white flannel jacket." At this time of sickness, he reportedly said that he was looking forward "with special joy" to gathering his impressions of Vienna: "I would stand at the street corner and let the stream of humanity rush past me, trying to grasp even the slightest difference between these people and those whom I have observed before."[37] It is clear that he had come to Vienna with the intention of making literary use of such impressions. "Asked on his arrival, if he would work in Vienna, he answered: 'I am a diligent man, a year must be used.' " And upon then being asked if he expected to work on a Viennese topic, he replied, "Certainly, Vienna is such an interesting place that at any rate something—I cannot say yet what it may be—will force itself upon my mind and ask to be worked upon."[38]

It was an accurate prediction. Something in Vienna did soon capture his interest. Exciting political events were in progress, and he became intensely absorbed in following them. Lederer has recorded:

> A short time after his arrival Mark Twain attended a session of the City Council of Vienna. He took a seat in the press gallery where he had a good view of the magnificent hall which he much admired. Dr. Karl Lueger, then Mayor of Vienna, was at the same time President of the City Council. He was the leader of the Anti-Semitic Christian Social Party, which had its supporters mainly among the lower middle classes, and had come to power after brutally smashing all resistance, even that of the Crown. He had to be elected three times by making use more of demagogic than of democratic methods before his election got the sanction of the monarch.
>
> The fact that only the Mayor spoke during the proceedings struck him as odd, and he asked ironically if the councillors were not permitted to speak as well. . . . At the close, Mark Twain remarked with "a peculiar smile," that he had been much interested in the session.[39]

Twain had also the opportunity of observing Dr. Lueger in the sessions of the Reichsrath, or Imperial Parliament, of which this demagogic mayor was a member. The Reichsrath was having turbulent times as a result of a recent shift in the balance of power. He started covering its sessions as a kind of reporter-at-large for America.[40] Notebook entries that he made in November, 1897, include lengthy memoranda of proceedings, with the hour and minute noted in some instances.[41] On November 4, Twain was present at one of the more riotous sessions, during which Dr. Otto Lecher made a historic twelve-hour speech and Dr. Lueger also spoke. The *Neue Freie Presse* reported Twain's reactions, as here summarized by Lederer:

> Mark Twain was all attention, watching the turbulent events with intense interest. He was shown those members of Parliament whose names were known to him through the newspapers. . . . At length Mark Twain drew out his notebook from his pocket and began to put down his . . . impressions of the uproar. An expression of greatest astonishment appeared on

his face when a chorus of yelling voices and hammering the wooden desks with bare fists and all kinds of instruments filled the noble ampitheatre. . . . He stared down into the hall as if something was happening there which he had believed impossible. . . . Mark Twain who had come before the session opened remained seated in his place taking notes as late as 11 p.m.[42]

It is evident that he believed he was seeing history made before his eyes, and that he missed little of the spectacle, of which he wrote in "Stirring Times in Austria," a masterful exposition of complex political events.[43] These happenings had an impact upon his composition of "Eseldorf." To begin with, it can be shown that three of his story characters were given names of actual persons who had played prominent roles in the Reichsrath meetings and had thus figured as important characters in the dramatic incidents that he described in "Stirring Times." One of these legislators was Deputy Wohlmeyer, whose name is found in "Eseldorf" (and in *The Mysterious Stranger*) as that of Theodor's comrade Seppi Wohlmeyer. Another was Vice President Fuchs, whose name occurs in the story as that of a wealthy young brewer, Joseph Fuchs. (The latter appears as a disappointed suitor in a long passage, deleted from the published tale, in which the young ladies of the village fall in love with young Satan, the mysterious stranger.) The third person, who was especially prominent in the events that led to the outbreak of rioting on the floor of the assembly, was Dr. Karl Lueger, leader of the anti-Jewish Christian Socialist Party and Burgomeister of Vienna.[44]

The manuscript shows that in beginning "Eseldorf," Twain at first called one of his characters "Father Lueger." He then began writing "Adolf" in place of "Lueger" a few pages before he reached the end of the first chapter; thereafter he went back and substituted the new name wherever he had already written "Lueger."[45]

There is reason to think that the impression he gained of Dr. Karl Lueger inspired his characterization of Father Lueger, as well as his initial choice of that name. What his appraisal of Dr. Lueger would have been may be readily inferred from the representation of him by the *Britannica* as the leader of "a clerico-anti-Semitic Tammany in Vienna."[46] It will be recalled that he soon thereafter championed the Jewish people in his essay "Concerning the Jews,"[47] and that some three years later he was to lead a vigorous attack upon New York's Tammany.[48] There can be little doubt that he conceived a strong dislike for Dr. Lueger, regarding him as a conniving opportunist, a politico-religious power-seeker.[49] In his notebook he recorded his impression that "the clever Lueger is a graceful man & most persuasive *looking* speaker—and probably *is* a competently bitter one."[50] In the "Stirring Times" article he described Lueger as one who knew how to "trim his sails to any wind," and, sardonically, as "that distinguished religious expert."[51] He also reported the remarks of those who styled Lueger as "the shifty trickster of Vienna"[52] and "Betrayer of the People."[53] It is therefore of particular significance that in the "Eseldorf" version the priest who was initially called "Father Lueger" is a thoroughly bad priest, a greedy, power-seeking hypocrite. Some of the bad priest's activities, as represented by Twain, probably had direct reference to events in which the actual Dr. Lueger had figured. Here is a likely example. The Austrian elections of 1895 had resulted in a sweeping victory for the anti-Jewish faction. In October of that year, the municipal council of Vienna had elected Dr. Lueger as mayor. He thereupon became the leader of his party, displacing the former leader Prince Liechtenstein, whose policies had been more acceptable to the emperor.[54] These events may be related to Twain's statement, which appears in "Eseldorf" and in *The Mysterious Stranger* near the end of Chapter I, that the good priest "Father Peter had been out a couple of years, and our other priest, Father Adolf [Twain first wrote Lueger] had his flock."[55] By the fall of 1897, it was literally true that the (good) Prince Liechtenstein had been out for some two years and that Dr. Lueger "had his flock." A further consideration is that Mark Twain was on visiting terms with the royal family and sympathetic to their side of the political contest in which Dr. Lueger was leading the opposition. A notebook entry of Sunday, October 10, 1897, reported that he had discussed with the princess the harm done by priests when they meddled in politics.[56] It is likely that their remarks included oblique, if not direct, references to Dr. Lueger.

It is necessary to explain that the bad priest has been edited almost entirely out of the published version. He was, as the manuscript clearly reveals, intended by Twain as the villain of the tale, the one who falsely accused Father Peter of stealing money from him, gave false testimony at the trial, and committed many other misdeeds. Whereas in the published story he is initially described merely as "a very zealous and strenuous priest, much considered,"

Twain actually described Father Lueger at this point as "a very loud and zealous and strenuous priest . . . always working to get more reputation," and added, satirically, that "he was dissolute and profane and malicious but otherwise a good enough man, it was generally thought."[57] Furthermore, it appears that A. B. Paine and F. A. Duneka, who shared the work of editing the story for publication, actually invented another character, the astrologer, whom Twain did not have in the story, and attributed to him the villainies of the bad priest that could not be deleted without destroying the plot. In the original typescript that was prepared for use as the printer's copy, derogatory references to the bad priest have been systematically put upon the astrologer—often simply by substituting "the astrologer" for the other name. For example, in the published text Nikolaus observes, "Father Peter, with the exception of the astrologer you haven't a real enemy in the village."[58] However, the manuscript, as well as the typescript before editing, had read ". . . with the exception of Father Adolf."[59] When necessary, more extensive rewriting was done to effect the substitution. Once these matters are understood, the connection between Twain's adverse impression of Dr. Lueger and his strongly unfavorable characterization of Father Lueger (Adolf) becomes sufficiently evident. It may be considered that in writing "Stirring Times in Austria," a work of literary journalism, he had had to try to remain objective, or nearly so. He did, as has been shown, find opportunity to quote several disparaging remarks that had been directed at Dr. Lueger, and had in one or two places brought in his own satirical touches, as when in mock praise he had termed him "that distinguished religious expert." But these hits were surely mild and decorous in comparison to the manner in which he would have wished to vent his rage or scorn upon this leader of a "clerico-anti-Semitic Tammany." In a tale such as *The Mysterious Stranger,* he could fully let himself go in vituperative denunciation.

Some working notes that he made for the beginning of "Eseldorf" may indicate that a need to have his full say against Lueger furnished the impetus which carried him into composition. These notes, which are on a single sheet of paper matching that of the first part of the manuscript and which are especially relevant to the dating of Mark Twain's composition of it, are here presented. They were originally made in pencil; later, in black ink, most of the deletions (shown in brackets) and additions (shown in italics) were made. It will be seen that he began with a hostile description of Lueger (his subsequent assigning of this name to a girl character will be explained later):

Plenty Jews

[Father] *Marie* Lueger, a drinking, spiteful, prying, over-godly, malicious priest. Supplanter of Kitchelt

Father Kitchelt (Block)
Margarethe (niece)
Nikolaus (Nick) Baumann [(Huck)] *Tom Sawyer* [*master miller's*]
               son of judge
Seppi Wohlmeyer [(Pole)] *good but simple the innkeeper's*
Theodor Fischer [*Tom*] *Huck* (I.   *—sexton, organist, leader of*
 Son of Hans   *the village band, commune tax collector*
          & some other things.

Wilhelm Meidling (Tom Andrews)
The Bishop
      Philip Traum
Procession to quiet Satan (table rapping)
Bridge—Satan built it)
   B. Langenan's tale of the Virgin—
   Wayside shrines—crown & nails and paint
   Old women and dogs harnesed—and carrying bricks & mortar

The great noble Prince—owner of the estate. His hunting-stags destroy crops. The forester (game-keeper)

Village [Hasenfeld] Eseldorf	Castle on heights—precipice—long
Castle park wide	winding road to it—it overlooks
Other sid [*Sic*] river in a rich plain,	river—boats & rafts. With garden
monkery in a grove.	in front on bank.

			Ghetto
	New Jerusalem		Jew
Stephan	Lehrer	I.	Goldschmid[t]
Edmund	Herold	I.	Nussbaum
	Bochner		Blumenduft[60]

Several things may be learned from these notes. First, it is evident that they were made after Mark Twain had been attending the Reichsrath sessions, but while their events were still fresh in his mind. Indeed, the characterization of Lueger as "drinking, spiteful, prying, over-godly, malicious," which closely parallels that of him in the story as "dissolute and profane and malicious," suggests that he both made the notes and began composition while his adverse impression of the actual Dr. Lueger was so strong and compelling that he had to write about it. The name "Wohlmeyer" which also appears here as well as in the story, further shows that he was finding material in his experience of the parliamentary meetings, in which a person so named had figured. Also, the last items on the sheet, consisting of listed names headed "New Jerusalem" placed opposite those headed "Ghetto/Jew," are probably references to the anti-Semitism that had been a prominent aspect of those proceedings. In a letter of October 23, 1897, to J. H. Twichell, he had reported that he found "much politics agoing," and that it was "Christian and Jew by the horns."[61] All of this evidence reinforces the consideration that he wrote these working notes and very likely began the story not long after his viewing of those historic sessions of the Austrian parliament, which continued until November 26, when an uprising caused the suspension of parliamentary government.[62]

Second, the notes contain other items which confirm that they were, in fact, made for and before the writing of the beginning of "Eseldorf." The setting that is briefly sketched—"Castle on heights—precipice—long winding road to it—it overlooks river—boats & rafts"—was used at the start of the story as that of the village of Eseldorf, with its "vast castle" that frowned from the top of a "lofty precipice," beyond which "flowed the tranquil river."[63] And it is noteworthy that alongside this setting he wrote "Village Hasenfeld" and then, in the same pencil-writing, struck out "Hasenfeld" and inserted "Eseldorf." That the change was made in pencil, not in ink as were other revisions, makes it seem likely that he changed the name almost immediately after putting down "Hasenfeld" (i.e., Rabbitfield). And, nominally speaking, when this change was made, the "Eseldorf" version as such was originated.

Third, most of the items that Twain added in black ink were apparently noted after he had written the first chapter but before he began the second. Several additions provided the backgrounds of the three principal boy-characters, who had not figured much in the initial, "Lueger-inspired" chapter. At the start of Chapter II, this material was used, with some elaboration. Nikolaus, designated in the notes as "son of judge," became "son of the principal judge of the local court"; Seppi, noted as "the innkeeper's [son]," became "son of the keeper of the principal inn." And in a similar fashion Twain followed his notes in describing Theodor as "son of the church organist, who was also leader of the village musicians, teacher of the violin, composer, tax-collector of the commune, sexton."[64] Also added in black ink was "Philip Traum," the name that was to be assumed by the young Satan in Chapter II. And "Father" was deleted and "Marie" inserted before "Lueger." He had already changed the name of the bad priest to "Adolf" before he had finished writing the first chapter; while reviewing his notes he evidently shifted the original name to the girl-character who bears it in the published story as well as in the manuscript as the only surviving usage of "Lueger": at the end of Chapter IV, it is related that Father Peter's niece Marget was "at the spinnet teaching Marie Lueger."[65] Marie is described as an "influential" pupil, without any explanation of the source of her influence. Twain may at first have intended to present her as the niece of the powerful Father Lueger.

Fourth, the notes reveal that he was actually planning the story as an adaptation of a previously written draft, a few pages of which he was to include, with revisions, in "Eseldorf." By adding the names "Huck," "Pole," and "Tom Andrews," he was identifying several characters of the earlier draft with those he now planned to call by other names. There are nineteen pages of "Eseldorf" in which, as they were originally written, one of the boys was regularly called "Huck"; this name was later deleted and "Nikolaus" inserted. By similar changes "Pole" became "Seppi" and "Tom Andrews" became "Wilhelm Meidling" (the latter is Father Peter's lawyer and Marget's suitor). Likewise, the good preacher of the "pre-Eseldorf" draft, a "Mr. Block," became "Father Peter" by Twain's revision.[66]

Before such changes had been made, these pages had told of Mr. Block's finding of a fortune of "eleven hundred dollars-odd!" which a young Satan had made to appear in his path, and of his agreeing —after much persuasion by Huck and his comrades—to keep the money.[67] As the presence of Huck in the story suggests, this earlier draft had an American setting. It was probably written before Twain's creative imagination had been influenced by the Austrian events that, as has been shown, soon found their way into "Eseldorf." Inasmuch as the letter of October 23 which has already been quoted is mostly about Austrian politics, a likely conjecture is that he had already written, some time previously, the "pre-Eseldorf" pages. Just when he did write them is uncertain; however, the evidence of the materials indicates that he probably did not do so until he had come to Vienna. These pages are on the same paper as that of the rest of the first eighty-five "Eseldorf" pages and of ten additional ones originally numbered 84-93 but later repaginated 377-386. The notes for the beginning of "Eseldorf" are, as has been mentioned, also on this paper. As it happens, this particular paper —of heavy, buff sheets, size $5\frac{1}{4}''$ by $8\frac{3}{8}''$—seems to have been used only during the first few months of Twain's stay at Vienna; a systematic search of the manuscripts has revealed no use of it at other times. In particular, it is significant that none of it is to be found in the manuscripts he is known or believed to have written while at Weggis, where he stayed for more than two months before going to Austria.[68] It is likely, then, that he composed the "pre-Eseldorf" draft some time within the first several weeks following his arrival in Vienna. If he did write it then, he would at the time of making notes for beginning "Eseldorf" have still had his first set of characters well in mind—as seems to have been the case.

3

ONCE IT IS KNOWN that Mark Twain began the writing of "Eseldorf" near the end of 1897, it becomes possible to identify some of the preliminary steps that he had taken toward such composition. It is necessary to go back a little in order to consider a few of these earlier stages of the creative process.

To seek the real beginning, the "germ" of the tale, is to be confronted with a variety of only partly satisfactory choices. For example, it could be said that Twain in his own boyhood, as Sam Clemens of Hannibal, was the original of the mysterious stranger. His great-nephew Samuel Charles Webster has recorded that Sam's mother, Jane Clemens (who had named her first son Orion for "the constellation under which he was born"), was a devotee of the occult:

> To the end of her days anything mystic intrigued her, and when she was an old lady in Fredonia, New York, there was nothing she enjoyed more than the visits from her doctor who was a Spiritualist. . . . Jane Clemens always answered his questions about her ailments as fast as possible so that she would have time to hear the latest news from the spirit world.69

This lady, "who was perhaps the strongest influence on his life,"70 would naturally have inclined the gifted and impressionable Sam toward her interests. "As a boy," Webster relates, "Uncle Sam was supposed to be a mind reader," and many times "the neighbors were invited in and entertained by him."71 Also, the boy had strange dreams and premonitions, was a good subject for mesmerism, and was known to be a somnambulist. Was not young Sam already living the part of Philip Traum, who in *The Mysterious Stranger* would entertain and astonish others with mind reading exhibitions and other mental feats? In a sense, he was;

yet those early experiences, however relevant to his eventual composition, did not in themselves represent the beginning of a story.[72]

Conceivably, Mark Twain first entertained the idea of writing the work that became *The Mysterious Stranger* on or shortly after November 6, 1895, when he was in New Zealand. He then noted:

> It is the strangest thing that the world is not full of books that scoff at the pitiful world, and the useless universe and violent, contemptible human race—books that laugh at the whole paltry scheme and deride it. Curious, for millions of men die every year with these feelings in their hearts. Why don't *I* write such a book? Because I have a family. There is no other reason. Was this those other people's reason?[73]

In writing *The Mysterious Stranger,* he did produce such a book. Still, there is in this entry no indication of the plot and materials that he thought of using; there is no *story*. Not until the beginning of 1897 does there appear to be any real hint that he had perhaps conceived the story-idea, or at least an essential part of it.

At Christmastime in 1896, he had noted that he was reading "Apparitions of the Living."[74] Probably the book was *Phantasms of the Living,* the early classic study of psychic phenomena, which reported upon the investigations of the Society for Psychical Research.[75] He had long been interested in such matters and had written of them in "Mental Telegraphy," in which he had stated, "Ever since the English Society for Psychical Research began its investigations of ghost stories, haunted houses, and apparitions of the living and the dead, I have read their pamphlets with avidity as fast as they arrived."[76] In *Phantasms of the Living,* he would have found much discussion of apparitions, materializations and dematerializations, clairvoyance, telepathy, precognition, and dream experiences. A few days later, on January 7, 1897, he made an extensive set of notes regarding a "spiritualized self which can detach itself and go wandering off upon affairs of its own," an

> other and wholly independent personage who resides in me—and whom I will call Watson, for I don't know his name, although he most certainly has one, and signs it in a hand which has no resemblance to mine when he takes possesion of our partnership body and goes off on mysterious trips —but I *am* acquainted (dimly) with my spiritualized self and I know that it and I are one, because we have common memory; when I wake mornings, I remember . . . whither it (that is *I*) have been wandering in the course of what I took to be unreality and called Dreams, for want of a truthfuller name.

> Now, as I take it, my other self, my dream self, is merely my ordinary body and mind freed from clogging flesh and become a spiritualized body and mind and with the ordinary powers of both enlarged in all particulars a little, and in some instances prodigiously.[77]

The powers here attributed to the dream self are similar to those of the boy-Satan of "Eseldorf," who possesses virtually unlimited mental capabilities. His earthly name, Philip Traum, also signifies that he is in some sense a dream person. And he first appears in the story after Theodor and his friends had spent much of the night talking of ghosts and angels and sudden dissappearances:

> It was after that kind of a talk one May night that we got up next morning and had a good breakfast . . . and went away up into the hills on the left to a woody hill-top which was a favorite place of ours, and there we stretched out on the grass in the shade to rest and smoke and talk over these strange things, for they were in our minds yet, and impressing us. . . .
>
> Soon there came a youth strolling toward us through the trees.[78]

It is, of course, the mysterious stranger. The timing of his appearance suggests that he is something like a hallucination resulting from particularly vivid dreams (or, conceivably, wakeful nighttime imaginings), and that he is closely akin to the dream-self Watson, whose marvelous actions Twain would have in mind upon awakening. In this connection, it is of interest that he had also been reading, about two months previously, William James's *The Principles of Psychology,* in which there is a discussion of hallucinations. One of James's observations is especially relevant:

> The world of dreams is our real world whilst we are sleeping, because our attention then lapses from the sensible world. Conversely, when we wake the attention usually lapses from the dream-world and that becomes unreal. *But if a dream haunts us and compels our attention during the day it is very apt to remain figuring in our consciousness as a sort of sub-universe alongside of the waking world.* Most people have probably had dreams which it is hard to imagine not to have been glimpses into an actually existing region of being, perhaps a corner of the "spiritual world."[79]

In particular the sentence for which italics have been supplied may be compared with Theodor's statement that the "strange things" of the past night were still in the boys' minds and were "impressing" the lads. That the dream would have had to be shared by several boys is perhaps no real difficulty. The thoughts and actions of the boys are not given any separate and individual presentation at this point: Theodor is allowed to speak for all of them, as though they have but one collective consciousness. His "we" seems here to be little more than a multiplied "I." Mark Twain needed more than one boy in order to convey a sense of community.

At the end of the notebook entry of January 7, it may be seen that he was already planning to use a self such as Watson as a story character: "The time that my dream self first appeared to me and explained itself (apparently I was for the moment dreaming) it was as insubstantial as a dim blue smoke, and I saw the furniture through it, but it was dressed in my customary clothes."[80] Paine was no doubt right in commenting that this passage had about it "a touch of fiction."[81] And the apparitionlike insubstantiality of this dream entity is characteristic of Philip Traum's way of appearing and disappearing. After his first visit, he dissolves himself for the entertainment of his comrades: "He thinned away and thinned away until he was a soap-bubble, except that he kept his shape. You could see the bushes through him as clearly as you see things through a soap bubble."[82] It is not likely that Twain had, in January, 1897, as yet planned to represent his dream self as a young angel called Satan; however, it appears that he was working his way toward the conception of such a story character.

What his mood was during this genetic period is clear enough. The family had not celebrated Christmas that December; Twain had noted, "the name of the day was not mentioned."[83] They were thinking of Susy, who had died of meningitis four months earlier. In this time of grief, he found literary work a solace. On January 19, 1897, he wrote to the Rev. Joseph H. Twichell, his close friend during the Hartford years and afterward, "I work all the days, and trouble vanishes away when I use that magic. This book will not long stand between it and me, now; but that is no matter, I have many unwritten books to fly to for my preservation."[84] Similarly, he wrote to William Dean Howells five weeks later, on February 23, "I don't mean that I am miserable; no—worse than that, indifferent. Indifferent to nearly everything but work. I like that; I enjoy it, & stick to it." He represented himself as a dead person going through the motions of living: "Indeed I am a mud image, & it puzzles me to know what it is in me that writes, & has comedy-fancies & finds pleasure in phrasing them. It is a law of our nature, of course, or it wouldn't happen; the thing in me forgets the presence of the mud image & goes on its own way wholly unconscious of it & apparently of no kinship with it."[85] Here again is expressed the idea that he has another self, a more creative self. This alter ego seems not unlike the greatly empowered dream self discussed in the notebook passage. And it will be seen later that in *The Mysterious Stranger* Satan does, in some fashion, represent the creative power of the artist's unconscious mind.

Another part of the letter of February 23, referring to public events, reads, "These are sardonic times. Look at Greece, & that whole shabby muddle. But I am not sorry to be alive & privileged to look on. If I were not a hermit I would go to the House every day & see those people scuffle over it & blether about the brotherhood of the human race."[86] Later in the year, it has already been shown, he did look on at riotous sessions of the Austrian Parliament. His letter shows that he expected to derive a kind of wry satisfaction from seeing the "damned human race" expose itself; to a degree, his response to the sorry events of the Reichsrath sessions had already been conditioned. The mechanism that was to trigger the start of his composition of "Eseldorf" had been cocked and was waiting to be sprung.

His remarks concerning the "shabby muddle" in Greece referred to the Cretan revolt which was then taking place. Further references to outrageous actions in Crete at this time are to be found in his essay "The Lowest Animal," a diatribe on the baseness and worthlessness of man. This piece is full of the kind of denunciation that is also abundantly present in *The Mysterious Stranger*. There are many parallels, suggesting that he very likely referred to "The Lowest Animal" while composing the mysterious stranger's excoriations. Here are two comparisons:

"The Lowest Animal"	*The Mysterious Stranger*
1	
Man seems to be a rickety poor sort of thing, any way you take him; a kind of British Museum of infirmities and inferiorities. He is always undergoing repairs. A machine that was as unreliable as he is would have no market. On top of his specialty—the Moral Sense—are	. . . they [men] were so dull and ignorant and trivial and conceited, and so diseased and rickety, and such a shabby poor worthless lot all around.[88] Man is a museum of diseases, a home of impurities; he comes

piled a multitude of minor infirmities; such a multitude, indeed, that one may broadly call them countless.[87]

to-day and is gone to-morrow. . . . And man has the *Moral Sense*. You understand? He has the *Moral Sense*.[89]

2

Of all the animals, man is the only one that is cruel. He is the only one that inflicts pain for the pleasure of doing it. It is a trait that is not known to the higher animals. . . . Man is the Cruel Animal. He is alone in that distinction.[90]

. . . Man cannot claim to approach even the meanest of the Higher Animals. It is plain that he is constitutionally afflicted with a Defect which must make such approach forever impossible, for it is manifest that this defect is permanent in him, indestructible, ineradicable.

I find this Defect to be the *Moral Sense*. He is the only animal that has it. It is the secret of his degradation. It is the quality *which enables him to do wrong*. It has no other office. It is incapable of performing any other function. It could never have been intended to perform any other. Without it, man could do no wrong. He would rise at once to the level of the Higher Animals.[91]

It is like your paltry race— always lying, always claiming virtues which it hasn't got, always denying them to the higher animals, which alone possess them. No brute ever does a cruel thing— that is the monopoly of those with the Moral Sense. When a brute inflicts pain he does it innocently; it is not wrong; for him there is no such thing as wrong. And he does not inflict pain for the pleasure of inflicting it— only man does that. Inspired by that mongrel Moral Sense of his! A sense whose function is to distinguish between right and wrong, with liberty to choose which of them he will do. He is always choosing, and in nine cases out of ten he prefers the wrong. There shouldn't be any wrong; and without the Moral Sense there couldn't be any. And yet he is such an unreasoning creature that he is not able to perceive that the Moral Sense degrades him to the bottom layer of animated beings and is a shameful possession.[92]

It is evident that in "The Lowest Animal" he was shaping ideas that would find their way into "Eseldorf" and into *The Mysterious Stranger*.

According to DeVoto's note, "The Lowest Animal" "was to have been prefaced by newspaper clippings which apparently dealt with religious persecutions in Crete. The clippings have been lost."[93] Mark Twain, referring to those items, wrote that man cuts his neighbor's throat "if his theology isn't straight" and spoke of his being "at it today in Crete—as per the telegrams quoted above."[94]

The essay must accordingly have been written sometime before May 20, the date on which an armistice went into effect.

In June, 1897, he took a further step toward the writing of *The Mysterious Stranger*. On the 26th of that month, four days after he had witnessed Queen Victoria's Jubilee Celebration, Mark Twain wrote in his notebook, "Satan's boyhood—going around with other boys & surprising them with devilish miracles."[95] In thirteen words he had noted the basic plot-idea of *The Mysterious Stranger*. He seems not to have expressed the same idea in any earlier note, and this entry may be considered the essential fable that was to be developed, with much elaboration and complication, in the several versions.

There is no indication that he wrote any draft of the story at this time. To have done much writing just then would have been difficult, if not impossible, for during the next several weeks he made a brisk tour of Europe, visiting France, the Low Countries, and Germany.[96] Then, on July 18, having moved on to Switzerland, he took residence for the rest of the summer at Villa Bühlegg in the village of Weggis, beside Lake Lucerne.[97] In "Letters to Satan," produced at this time, he described his recent European travels, purportedly to induce Satan "to come out of . . . seclusion and make a pleasure tour through the world in person, instead of doing it by proxy through me."[98] This passage may furnish a hint that Twain was still holding in mind the notion of bringing Satan to earth as a story character—of having him tour the world in this sense, as indeed the boy-Satan does in *The Mysterious Stranger:* "We often went to the most distant parts of the globe with him,"[99] Theodor says.

On August 4, at Weggis, he began work on "Hellfire Hotchkiss," a story filled with characters, scenes, and events based on recollections of the village of his boyhood—Hannibal, Missouri, as he had known it in the 1840's.[100] After young Thug Carpenter ventures upon river ice just as it is breaking up, Hellfire saves him from what had seemed an inevitable—and fated—death by drowning.[101] This incident may be a foreshadowing of one in *The Mysterious Stranger,* wherein a similar situation is presented in an inverted form. What was to have been a foreordained rescue is changed to a drowning by the intervention of young Satan, who causes Theodor's friend Nikolaus to perish along with Lisa Brant in a futile attempt to rescue her (he confers the deaths as a kindness, knowing both had been destined to lead wretched lives).[102] However, "Hellfire Hotchkiss" is more directly related to the "Hannibal" draft than to the published version. Hellfire, the fiery and tempestuous tomboy of the village, actually figures as a character in "Hannibal": she and the mysterious stranger of that story were to fall in love—though Twain, it be seen later, abandoned the manuscript (written late in 1898) before giving much development to such a love-complication.

Most of the holograph of "Hellfire Hotchkiss" is on a paper that has a distinctive cross-barred pattern. There is very little of this stationery in the Mark Twain Papers, and Twain may very well have used it only while he was at Weggis. The manuscripts in which it was used have other similarities: there is the same dark ink (an intense black, which has resisted fading better than many of the inks that Twain used), and the handwriting (which was changing almost from year to year during this period) is in close agreement. "Villagers of 1840-1843," a 34-page sketch of Hannibal characters and of dramatic incidents in which they had figured, is one of these cognate manuscripts. Many of the noted events have tragic aspects. Drownings or near-drownings, for example, are mentioned several times. A tailor's apprentice is credited with having saved Simon Carpenter from drowning, and the latter is said to have cursed his rescuer for the next fifty years;[103] this incident seems to be related to the rescue of Thug Carpenter in "Hellfire Hotchkiss." And here, as in two other episodes in "Villagers," drowning is presented as a fortunate occurrence. At least one of these passages appears to be a close analogue of the incident of the drowning of Nikolaus and Lisa. It is related that Tom Nash, after falling through the ice, lost his speech and his hearing, and that his sisters were thereafter similarly afflicted as a result of scarlet fever.[104] In *The Mysterious Stranger,* Satan explains that he has really favored Theodor by changing a link in "the chain of his life":

> If I had not done this, Nikolaus would save Lisa, then he would catch cold from his drenching; one of your race's fantastic and desolating scarlet fevers would follow, with pathetic after-effects; for forty-six years he would lie in his bed a paralytic log, deaf, dumb, blind, and praying night and day for the blessed relief of death.[105]

It is not surprising that this incident was in all likelihood based on Twain's remembered Hannibal experiences, and that he was, while at Weggis, making an imaginative return to the village of his boyhood. During the past two years, he had been working under unusual pressure, first lecturing around the world and then applying himself to sustained work upon a lengthy travel book, the sale of which was to free him from debt.[106] Although he was still reading proof for *Following the Equator* during the first month at Weggis, he had finished the more demanding labor of composition in May. For the first time in a very long while, he was about to be free to undertake, without preoccupation, whatever writing might be of the greatest personal interest to him. It is understandable that he would have sought to renew his recollections of Hannibal and once again make use of those experiences which, as Henry Nash Smith has shown in "Mark Twain's Images of Hannibal: From St. Petersburg to Eseldorf," served him as a creative matrix during most of his years as a writer.[107]

On August 22 he wrote to Wayne MacVeagh that he had finished with the proofs and that he was a slave no longer. That morning, he said, he had planned four books. He expected to entertain himself by working on them during the next several years, shifting from one to another whenever it suited him to do so.[108] It will be recalled that in the preceding January he had written that he had "many unwritten books to fly to for . . . preservation"; he had then added that the time between the finishing of *Following the Equator* and the starting of his next book would "not be more than an hour, at most."[109] Significantly, he did at once commit himself to the writing of not one but four additional volumes after doing the last of his work upon the travel story. At this time he would have had much need for the "surcease of sorrow" that literary work could provide: four days earlier, on August 18, 1897, the anniversary of Susy's death had come. In the letter to MacVeagh, he spoke of the dark shadow of disaster that had again come over them and said that their tragic loss was still regarded in his family as a dream rather than a reality.[110] Considering Twain's somber mood, it seems likely that he was then preparing to create in terms of his "symbols of despair." Probably one of the four books planned on August 22 was *The Mysterious Stranger* in its earliest form—the "pre-Eseldorf" story.

The supposition that he had done some planning for the story of young Satan on August 22 gains support from further notebook entries that were made some time after that date and before

September 24, 1897. These "Notes for story—probably *The Mysterious Stranger,*" as Paine designates them, seem to be the observation of a Satanlike character speaking in disparagement of mankind and its pretensions:

> He had but one term for that large body which has such a fine opinion of itself—"the little stinking human race, with its little stinking kings and popes and bishops and prostitutes and peddlers."
> He said: "The globe is a living creature, and the little stinking human race and the other animals are the vermin that infest it—the microbes. We dig into its skin to suck its blood (water) and we use its Niagaras and rivers for power. We sail its oceans in fleets which it is not conscious of and cannot see. We dig deep into the thin outer gold-leaf layer of its skin, 3000 feet, and it is not aware of it. Nothing hurts it but a bellyache, then it heaves with a trifling earthquake."[111]

This noting of dialogue—or monologue—might indicate that he was either at work on the story or about to begin. But it is unlikely that he began the actual writing of the "pre-Eseldorf" draft until after he had moved to Vienna, during the last week of September.

It has already been mentioned that this draft and "Eseldorf" are written on the same kind of paper, a kind that he was not using at Weggis. Additional evidence that he could not, in any case, have carried the story far before his arrival in Vienna is furnished by some working notes that he made on two sheets of stationery bearing a printed heading, "Hotel Metropole, Wien, 189—."[112] These holographic notes have been written in black ink with a fine pen and in a handwriting matching the first part of "Eseldorf." The use of hotel stationery for his literary work was not at all his common practice; its use in this instance is one indication that he probably made the notes soon after coming to the Metropole, before he had supplied himself with other materials. However, the more telling fact is that in these notes there are no indications that his imagination had yet begun to concern itself with Austrian scenes and events.

An especially interesting feature of these "Metropole notes" is the inclusion of materials that later found their way into several of the other longer, principal manuscripts of the Despair Group, as well as items related to *The Mysterious Stranger.* These works may well be the four books that he had planned on August 22. He would hardly have developed these story ideas very much as yet. Conceived just after the anniversary of Susy's death, and having their common origin in the mood and viewpoint of Twain's despair, they may not have been very clearly differentiated. He had mapped out all of them during the same few morning hours. The notes contain just what one would expect to find soon afterward: Despair Group matter in gestation, with the different story lines distinguishable but not yet firmly segregated.

Several of the items are much in the vein of the notebook entries he had lately made in which a superhuman "He" compared the "little stinking human race" to microbes. Mention is made of a character named Ferg—apparently the same Ferguson who was to figure as a character in "3,000 Years Among the Microbes," a story featuring a cholera germ narrator who had, in a previous existence, been a man; Mark Twain carried this tale to a length of 40,000 words in 1905 before abandoning it.[113] Crazy Fields, who appears in the unpublished novel "Which Was Which?" (sometimes called the "George Harrison Story"),[114] is noted as having lost both his wife and his child after a friendless smallpox patient had been taken into his home. And there is a character who is to reveal his identity and then rescue some people from a storm; such an incident is found in the "Hannibal" version of *The Mysterious Stranger,* in which young Satan (or "44," as he is called in that draft) saves a number of villagers from a lethal snow storm. The snow, of paste-like consistency, clogs their eyes, ears, and nostrils; the people are amazed to find that "44" can survive in it and even see perfectly well in it, and his performance is considered miraculous. At least half of the notes do, however, seem to anticipate events of the "Eseldorf" version—although these happenings are presented without any Austrian coloring. The mysterious "He," for example, is credited with making instantaneous journeys to China, as Philip Traum does in "Eseldorf."[115] Another item, much like the one involving Crazy Fields, concerns a tragedy that results from a kindness done by the mother of Tom Nash: her children get scarlet fever from a homeless waif whom she takes in; three die, and two others are afflicted with deafness.[116] This episode recalls the one in "Villagers," mentioned earlier, involving Tom Nash, his sisters, scarlet fever, and deafness; it is also related to the previously quoted passage describing the life-plan of Nikolaus, who was to have contracted scarlet fever and then have suffered a loss of hearing.

Probably these working notes were made at about the time that Mark Twain began to write his earliest draft of *The Mysterious*

Stranger—not long after September 28, when he took quarters at the Metropole. The *Neue Freie Presse,* reporting on his activities shortly after his arrival, stated that although he was "under the immediate and strong impression of the strange city and wholly absorbed in this new experience, he was nevertheless occupied with writing an unfinished work."[117] It is likely that this work was the "pre-Eseldorf" story, with its Hannibal locale. One sees the creative momentum of the Hannibal-inspired effort suffering the counter-impact of the "strong impression" of Viennese events and losing its force. As Twain had foreseen, his new experiences soon became a compelling subject for literary work. It is evident that the impact of stirring times in Austria changed the course of his composition of *The Mysterious Stranger.* In the "Eseldorf" version, probably begun in November or December, he adapted the previous draft by introducing an Austrian setting and other Austrian material.

Perhaps his attendance of those historic meetings of the Reichsrath defined for him, more clearly than had any previous experience, the role of the detached, ironic observer looking down upon the follies and depravities of the human race and making his sardonic comments. It was a part that he was to continue playing. Within the next few years, as Paine has written, he came to be regarded not "merely as a humorist, but as a sort of Solon presiding over a court of final conclusions."[118] This role was, of course, also that of his mysterious stranger, who was a most appropriate persona for the later Mark Twain.

"Eseldorf," "Stirring Times in Austria," and "The Man That Corrupted Hadleyburg" all had a common origin in Twain's response to the events of his first two months in Vienna—particularly those that occurred on the floor of the Imperial Parliament. Paine appears to be correct in saying that "Hadleyburg" was "written during the winter of '97-'98," and in terming the story a "terrible arraignment of human weakness," in which "Mark Twain allowed himself to jeer at the species without restraint."[119] Paine's further comment, "Human hypocrisy and rotten moral force were never stripped so bare, never so mercilessly jeered at in the market-place,"[120] accurately describes the essential story-situation and reveals its close similarity to the situation of public exposure that Twain found in the parliamentary sessions. In "Hadleyburg," after a mysterious stranger has devised a plan for exposing the self-righteous and supposedly incorruptible town, the nineteen leading citizens all claim gold that is not rightfully theirs. At a town meeting, all are exposed save one (the guilt-tortured Richards, who later confesses). As these worthies are one by one revealed to be corrupt, their on-looking fellow villagers make derisive comments, very much, by Twain's report, as did those who witnessed the disgraceful actions of the legislators in the Reichsrath meetings. In the "Stirring Times" article, he had written: "A gallery witticism comes flitting by from mouth to mouth around the great curve: 'The swan-song of Austrian representative government!' You can note its progress by the applausive smiles and nods it gets as it skims along."[121]

Nineteen states, he had explained in "Stirring Times," were members of the Parliament, and there were "nineteen public opinions—one for each state."[122] And it is probably significant that there are nineteen principal townsmen in Hadleyburg, whom Twain pointedly calls the "Nineteeners."[123] The village is pre-sumably a microcosm of the Austro-Hungarian Empire and, by extension, of the entire world. It seems that he did not necessarily have Hannibal primarily in mind as the original of the village, and that Paine is again right in saying that "Hadleyburg had neither local geography nor circumstance, for Hadleyburg was the world, and Mark Twain, at sixty-three, having seen all the world and probed every human depth, had found some phase of the story's circumstance in every human soul."[124]

The part of "Eseldorf" that he wrote at this time parallels "Had-leyburg" and "Stirring Times" in its initial emphasis upon the tranquillity of the scene that is thereafter to become one of vio-lence and clamor when those who should represent the best of the human family dishonor themselves. Also, this part of the manu-script culminates in a courtroom scene, even as the principal action of "Hadleyburg" at the town hall assumes the aspect of a public trial and as an account of actions on the floor of the legislature constitutes the substance of "Stirring Times." Mark Twain was already presiding over his "court of final conclusions." Satan, of course, in a sense holds court throughout *The Mysterious Stranger*, as he examines, judges, and condemns the human race. In all three of these writings, humanity is confronted as it stands openly disgraced; the first reaction of those who look on is one of shock, and the one that soon follows manifests itself in cynical

snickers. And that is clearly the effect that Mark Twain intended.[125]

He was writing well. And it is noteworthy that Hannibal seems
not to have been the imaginative base of much of this writing. He
had found significant new material and an appropriate way of
treating it. He had, moreover, developed a new persona—one
representing his elder self; his sadder-and-wiser self; his *august*
self (it will be seen later that he called his "Print Shop" narrator
"August"). It may be granted that the role of a Solon or public
conscience could hardly have been a congenial one for Mark
Twain, as indeed it could not for anyone conceivably worthy of
such an office. But it is evident that a new surge of creative
power had been generated by the friction of momentous Austrian
events that had charged his thoughts; his artistic potential or
potency had seldom, since the 1880's, been greater. Probably it
was not because of any marked decline in talent that he did not
at this time write the rest of "Eseldorf" but discontinued work
upon it after writing about ninety-five pages.

It is entirely certain that he did not write all of the 423-page
"Eseldorf" version at this time; it will presently be shown that
there are in the latter part of it unmistakable references to his-
torical events of August, 1900. Thus, the problem is to determine
how long he continued his initial spurt of work upon the tale and
to what point he carried it. The available evidence weighs in
favor of his having taken it through that part which is on the buff
paper—pages 1-85 and 377-386 (originally 84-93). Inasmuch as he
used this paper in two other manuscripts that may be dated as of
late in 1897 or early in 1898,[126] but seems not to have used it
at any later time, it is likely that he wrote at this time all of
"Eseldorf" that is on these buff sheets.[126a] That he wrote no more
is suggested, though not proved, by the fact that the remaining
part is not only on different paper but differs also in its inks and
even in the handwriting (which changed markedly during Twain's
later years).[127] Additional support for these views is to be found
in the contents of pages 1-85 and 377-386, which in themselves present a story that has a unity and even a kind of completeness.
In the first eighty-five pages, he brought the story through the
beginning description of Eseldorf; the characterization of Father
Lueger (Adolf); the presentation of the other principal characters,
including the young Satan; the showing of the latter's wonderful

abilities and contempt for humanity; the finding of the gold coins by the needy good priest; the false accusation of Father Peter by the bad priest; and the extreme poverty suffered by Father Peter's household after his imprisonment. In the ten pages at first numbered 84-93, Twain carried the story at once into the trial scene, showing the bad priest's false testimony against his rival; the ineffectual defense attempted by Wilhelm Meidling; the subsequent discovery (prompted by Satan) that the coins had been minted too recently to have been in existence at the time of the supposed theft; the exoneration of the good priest; and, finally—as an ironic reversal—Satan's conferring insanity upon the latter as the only real and lasting happiness possible to a human being.[128] This portion of the manuscript might thus be considered a tale in itself. He had, it seems, written through to his denouement too quickly. He may have stopped work on the story at that time as a result of his not knowing just what else to do to keep his plot going.

He probably had laid the story aside before the middle of January, 1898. A notebook entry reads, *"Jan. 14, 1898.* Began to write comedy 'Is he Dead?' (Francois Millet.)"[129] And his letter of January 22, 1898, to William Dean Howells shows that he could very well have been working on *The Mysterious Stranger* just before beginning the play:

> I couldn't get along without work now. I bury myself in it up to the ears. Long hours—8 & 9 on a stretch, sometimes. And all the days, Sundays included. It isn't all for print, by any means, for much of it fails to suit me; 50,000 words of it in the past year. It was because of the deadness which invaded me when Susy died. But I have made a change lately—into dramatic work. . . .[130]

His words indicate clearly enough that during the earlier part of January he had been deeply absorbed in work upon one (or more) of his manuscripts of the Despair Group. In the light of the other evidence to the effect that he was working on "Eseldorf" at about this time, it is reasonable to think that he had been writing some of it during those "long hours."[131] Indeed, by working "all the days, Sundays included," he could have written all of the 12,350 words of the ninety-five buff pages during the first two weeks of January.[132] But it is likely that at least the initial chapter, so much of which is devoted to Lueger, had been written somewhat earlier and thus closer to the events that prompted its composition. Quite possibly he began writing "Eseldorf" on De-

cember 9, 1897. In a part of Chapter I that has been deleted
from the published text, it is related that the bad priest had even
schemed to cheat the devil out of a Christian that, according to
a pact, was to be his in return for the building of a bridge. The
previously quoted working notes evidently refer to such an incident: "Bridge—Satan built it." He had cleverly waited for word
of someone dying, so that he might deliver only a dead Christian:
"Towards midnight the 9th of December" the desired word was
brought, and the devil was summoned and required to provide the
bridge. Mark Twain, after dwelling upon the people's boundless
admiration of this trick, wrote that it was turned into a proud
ceremony "repeated every 9th of December, to this day."[133] The
pointed and iterated reference to the 9th of December may have
been a strictly contemporary one. In bringing "Stirring Times in
Austria" to an end, he had taken occasion to make a point of that
date, writing "We are well along in December now," and adding as
a footnote, "It is the 9th.—M.T."[134] His concluding remarks in
that essay had made it clear that he considered Austrian affairs
were in a state of crisis at that particular time—that they were
in fact in a deplorable and shameful condition. If, finding himself
free from other writing commitments, he did then plunge into the
composition of that first "Eseldorf" chapter, he would likely have
done just what he *has* done in it: employ satiric inversion and, in
mockery, celebrate this date as one marking events worthy of the
highest praise.

4

THERE IS NO INDICATION that, after writing the part of the manuscript that is on the buff-colored stationery, he did any more work on "Eseldorf" that winter, or indeed during the rest of 1898. It is true that there is a notebook entry, made in July of that year, which in irony praises the executive abilities of Satan "who for untold centuries has maintained the imposing position of spiritual head of 4/5 of the human race."[135] This passage was, however, used not in any version of *The Mysterious Stranger* but in "Concerning the Jews."[136] Furthermore, it can be shown that by November, 1898, he was planning and in all probability writing the "Hannibal" version.

His notebook contains the following entry of November 11-12, 1898:

> Story of little Satan Jr. who came to Hannibal, went to school, was popular and greatly liked by those who knew his secret. The others were jealous and the girls didn't like him because he smelled of brimstone. He was always doing miracles—his pals knew they were miracles, the others thought they were mysteries.[137]

Paine published only this beginning of the note, the full version of which runs to about five hundred words. The entry closely parallels sixteen pages of working notes, which have been designated as Group C.[138] These notes are a plot-summary for "Hannibal" as Twain probably intended to write it. He did not, however, carry the story as far as he had plotted for it. In fact, the manuscript amounts to little more than the start of the intended draft. In this beginning, the "little Satan" appears one morning at the village school and promptly startles everyone by giving his name as "44." He then performs astonishing feats of learning (such as incredibly rapid reading and infallible recall). After finding a home with the Hotchkiss family, he materializes himself at a spiritualist séance and then accomplishes other wonders such as rescuing many people from a terrible snowstorm. After explaining about his ancestry, he summons a little devil to serve Mr. Hotchkiss. At this point the manuscript breaks off.[139] According to the plot, "44" was to walk through fire to save a child and then come out unharmed after the burning building had fallen in upon him. He was to explain that he couldn't feel any kind of pain and that he believed it to be imaginary. He was thereafter to fall in love with the pastor's daughter, and to try to convince her father that all human actions are prompted by selfishness. And he was to go to church and by and by get converted and become a Methodist, only to be put out of the church after he had been caught praying for Satan, his father. Later on, "44" was to decide to rid man of the Moral Sense, so that the race might be guiltless and happy; to this end, he was to start his own Anti-Moral Sense Church and to have his little devil brothers print his "bible" for him—proclaiming such ideas as Mark Twain expressed in *What Is Man?* (which in his later years he often termed his "gospel"). Also, "44" was to fall in love with Hellfire Hotchkiss (possibly Twain intended this episode as an alternate for the one involving the preacher's daughter) and get more than he had bargained for, finding that the intellectualized love of immortals was tame in comparison to earthly love.[140]

There is no evidence to show that Twain ever wrote any more of "Hannibal" than now survives. Containing only about 15,300 words, this manuscript would have required perhaps not quite two weeks of work at his usual pace. That he did this writing soon after making the notebook entry concerning little Satan, Jr., is suggested by the fact that page 5 of Group C of the working notes has on the reverse side an uncompleted letter by Twain to Henry H. Rogers, dated November 17, 1898. There is a probability that he was drafting these notes at about that time, only a few days after the entry of November 11-12. He would thus have been at work upon "Hannibal" either at that time or shortly thereafter, writing it in the latter part of November, and perhaps the early part of December, 1898. It is hard to say why he carried the draft no further. It may be of significance that he had tried to write "Hannibal" from the omniscient point of view, rather than that of a boy-narrator. Tom and Huck never really came into the story, in the fragment that he wrote, except as mere allusions. He may have found that they did not belong in the same story with the phantom-boy, Philip Traum, and could not be made to associate with him. Or perhaps Mark Twain, the Solon of an unofficial world "court of final conclusions," could no longer write from the viewpoint of a boy—a real boy, as Sam Clemens of Hannibal had been. In creating Philip Traum he had found a character who could be at once a youth and a sage: an angel-boy sixteen thousand years old.[141] Satan, Jr., who comes off mainly as an unusually brilliant schoolboy in the "Hannibal" manuscript, probably did not so well meet Twain's literary needs.[142] In any case, it is evident that he had made another start upon the story of a young Satan but had not found it to be the right one. These facts take on an added significance when related that what he wrote to Howells on May 12-13, 1899. Reporting that he was working on "a book without reserves" in which he meant to say his say and "take account of no one's feelings, no one's prejudices, opinions, beliefs, hopes, illusions, delusions," he explained:

> Twice I didn't start it right; & got pretty far in both times, before I found it out. But I am sure it is started right this time. It is in [story] tale-form. I believe I can make it tell what I think of Man, & how he is constructed, & what a shabby poor ridiculous thing he is, & how mistaken he is in his estimate of his character & powers & qualities & his place among the animals.
>
> So far, I think I am succeeding. I let the madam into the secret day before yesterday, & locked the doors & read to her the opening chapters. She said—
>
> "It is perfectly horrible—and perfectly beautiful!"
>
> "Within the due limits of modesty, that is what I think."
>
> I hope it will take me a year or two to write it, & that it will turn out to be the right vessel to contain all the ordure I am planning to dump into it.[143]

His comment that he had twice started wrong and had twice gotten "pretty far in" seems an apt reference to his writing of the initial 12,350 words of "Eseldorf" and of the 15,300 words of "Hannibal" in his previous attempts at telling the tale that was to become *The Mysterious Stranger*. To be sure, if the "pre-Eseldorf" draft were to be counted as a separate version, the number would be three; but inasmuch as he had adapted it for "Eseldorf" and had even inserted some of its pages, he might very well have thought of both drafts as just one try at getting the story told.

It may be further considered that at some time he had to set aside the ten pages written on the buff sheets (84-93) and then write almost three hundred additional pages of "Eseldorf" before bringing in the deferred portion as pages 377-386. It seems likely that what he did in May, 1899, to get the tale "started right" was to reserve for later use that part in which he had used up his plot much too quickly in presenting the trial of Father Peter and its ironic—and tragic—outcome.

This interpretation is supported by the evidence of a single page of working notes, on paper matching that of pages 86-376 and 387-392 of "Eseldorf," which is clearly his plan for continuing the story from the point to which it had been carried in the first eighty-five pages. The first several items read:

> S. will come "every day."
> Jealousy of Wil.
> S. after 3 days furnishes details of the 4 games, with notes to Wil, whose envy & jeal are further inflamed.[144]

On page 85, the tale had reached the point at which Father Peter had been put in jail and his family had been left without support. Although momentary relief had been provided by a coin that the housekeeper Ursula had been given for washing, or attempting to wash, some clothes, and that she had thereafter pretended she had found in the road, she "could not find a coin in the road every day—perhaps [the sentence is completed on page 86, on a cream-colored paper and in a gray ink] not even a second one." In the next paragraph, Satan comes again—as he does repeatedly thereafter; he soon has the lucky cat, Agnes, providing "four silver groschen . . . every morning."[145] Thereafter, Satan exhibits to the village boys many instances of human cruelty while preaching to them a continuing sermon on the degrading effect of man's "Moral Sense."[146] In this material Mark Twain seems to be speaking without reserve in the way that he had contemplated in the letter to Howells of May 12-13. Apparently he was drawing upon "The Lowest Animal" for story material. Probably it was that satiric essay, written in the spring of 1897 at the time of the revolt in Crete, that he had had in mind when he told Howells that he was planning to "dump" much "ordure" into his tale.

After such material had actually been dumped into the story, he needed additional subject matter. In his working notes he had referred to the jealousy of Wilhelm. He next developed this plot-element in the long passage (about eight thousand words, mostly deleted from *The Mysterious Stranger*) in which Wilhelm and the brewer Joseph Fuchs become intensely jealous of Satan. The latter captivates the girls Marget and Lilly by reciting marvelous poetry, getting splendid orchestral effects out of a tuneless old piano, and effortlessly defeating Wilhelm in chess—even though Wilhelm is the champion of that region. And to cap his performance, Satan, as Twain had planned, makes Wilhelm even more envious by later setting down from memory, in an instant's time and with perfect accuracy, the records of their games.[147]

That it was at the time of this continuation of the story that he put aside the ten pages presenting the trial scene is confirmed by the last item appearing on this same sheet of working notes:

> Trial of Peter—he not present. Is begged by the boys to go & confer an immense happiness upon him to pay for his captivity & make him forget it. He confers a happy insanity—imaginary kingship. Will not restore him—*knows* a happy insanity is best for all men. . . .[148]

He was here looking forward to using, only after writing through the rest of his noted plot-ideas, a trial scene which he had almost certainly written before making these notes. He had probably recognized that, by delaying this outcome, he was making it possible to indulge in any amount of digressive moralizing and yet make the plot come out as he intended. He had a "finisher" laid by and waiting. He might well have felt sure that this time his story was "started right."

Some evidence makes it appear probable that by the fall of 1899 he had written through the part devoted to the love-rivalry theme, but not much further. A very little of this sequence has survived in the published tale: in the middle of Chapter VII it is related that Satan charmed Marget when he "branched off into poetry, and recited some," but that "Wilhelm was not as pleased as he ought to have been, and this time Marget noticed it and was remorseful."[149] It is from here that "Eseldorf" continues with nearly eight thousand words, all deleted before publication, in which Satan further arouses the love of Marget and Lilly and the jealousy of their beaux. Twain had, in writing to the end of this plot-sequence, reached a total of about 29,500 words in the manuscript. The figure agrees well enough with one which he reported in what is probably a reference to his work upon "Eseldorf," in his letter to Howells of October 19, 1899:

> Ah, if I could look into the insides of people as you do, & put it on paper, & invent things for them to do & say, & tell *how* they said it, I could write a fine & readable book now, for I've got a prime subject. I've written 30,000 words of it & satisfied myself that the stuff is there; so I am going to discard that MS & begin all over again & have a good time with it.150

In writing the love-and-jealousy episodes, he had apparently lost the thread of what little plot he had had going. It is true that he had brought a little of the same kind of material into the initial part of "Eseldorf"—mainly in the pages that he had retained from the Hannibal-oriented "pre-Eseldorf" draft. Theodor, he had written, had "passed through the parlor," finding Marget at the piano giving a lesson to Marie Lueger.151 And in the garden he had found "Wilhelm Meidling sitting there waiting, for it was getting toward the edge of evening, and he would be asking Marget to take a walk along the river with him when she was done with the lesson. He was a young lawyer, and succeeding fairly well and working his way along, little by little. He was very fond of Marget, and she of him."152 For these scenes, Twain was very likely using recollections of the Clemens household at about 1850 (when he was in his fifteenth year). Samuel C. Webster is no doubt right in thinking that this passage in *The Mysterious Stranger* is based upon memories of the kind of home life described in Jane Clemens' letter of January 30, 1850, to Orion:

> Since I commenced writing an invitation came for Pamela to spend the evening out but she is in the dining room giving Margaret Blesser a lesson on the Guitar, Sarah Fuqua and I are in the parlour, Sarah is pract[ic]ing and I writing. . . . Tomorrow evening the music scollars meet again. Margaret Saxon, Sara Fuqua and Mary Buckhannan all play dewets, the scollars are improving very fast. When you come I think they will play well.153

Webster comments that "Sam, coming back from the printing house for an evening at home, must often have seen the picture of Pamela and her scholars that Jane Clemens describes."154 In carrying the story of "Eseldorf" to almost thirty thousand words, Mark Twain introduced a great deal more matter of this kind. It seems that he had again tried to use Hannibal material and had found that the attempt did not work out very well. Satan, when placed in the social context of the author's own village, tended to become a bright and talented lad who pleased the girls with parlor tricks—very much as "44," the young Satan of the "Hannibal" version, had shown himself to be a schoolboy paragon. Certainly the mood, tone, and subject matter of this attempt in 1899 were not in keeping with the greater part of the beginning portion of "Eseldorf." He might well have seen that the story was floundering; that he needed to "invent things" for his characters "to do & say." It would not have been surprising had he then thought of discarding the manuscript and starting again. And it appears that he did make some plans for a rewriting of "Eseldorf." There are five pages of working notes in which it may be seen that he was reviewing pages 1 to 85, which he had written almost three years previously: he noted the characters and incidents along with the pages upon which they appear and added his plans for further development of many episodes. For example, at the point at which Satan fashions the tiny castle which he thereafter destroys, Twain noted, "Make him build a whole city and then drown it with a bucket of water."[155] But these revisions were never made, and the contents of the following part of the story show that he presently found a new impetus which prompted him to continue the existing manuscript instead of beginning anew. Immediately after the love-rivalry passage, a new plot-sequence is initiated in which there soon begin to appear references to contemporary events that probably, and in some cases certainly, could not have been made before the summer of 1900.

At once, Satan takes Theodor to China. And there is this curious allusion to current happenings—or rather what seems to stop just short of being that:

> It was wonderful, the spectacles we saw; and some were beautiful, others too horrible to think. For instance—However, I may go into that by and by, and also why Satan chose China for this excursion instead of another place; it would interrupt my tale to do it now.[156]

The author virtually tells the reader outright that outrageous things are going on in China at the time of writing. He does not say enough about them to make a positive identification possible. But it is evident that the reference would fittingly apply to the Boxer uprising—particularly to the extremes of violence that occurred during the latter part of June and the early part of July, 1900, when China was invaded by international troops and, by order of the Empress Dowager, hundreds of foreigners (chiefly missionaries) were slain.[157] Before following up his first cryptic comment upon the situation in China, Twain wrote an additional 9,200 words of "Eseldorf" (as he had given notice he would do rather than "interrupt" his story).[158] Then, by having Satan show Theodor and Seppi a vision of the history of mankind, including an exhibition of the future, Twain found his chance for contemporary allusions.[159] Much of this material has not survived editing; that which was retained does, however, include Satan's sardonic prophecy that "the pagan world will go to school to the Christian not to acquire his religion, but his guns," and that "the Chinaman will buy those to kill missionaries and converts with."[160] In the deleted portion, the reference is more explicit: the Chinese, it is said, after becoming exasperated by foreign interference will "rise in revolt against the insults and oppressions of the intruder. This will be Europe's chance to interfere and swallow China, and her band of royal Christian pirates will not waste it."[161] Some sixty-three pages later, Satan is still predicting the future in a similar fashion, with probable reference to both the Boer War and the occupation of China by the Allied Powers: "Two centuries from now . . . the Christian civilization will reach its highest mark. Yet its kings will still be, then, what they are now, a close corporation of land-thieves."[162] The references to events in China may be compared with Twain's letter to J. H. Twichell of August 12, 1900, in which he spoke of recent news reports:

> It is all China, now, and my sympathies are with the Chinese. They have been villainously dealt with by the sceptered thieves of Europe, and I hope they will drive all the foreigners out and keep them out for good. I only wish it; of course I don't really expect it.[163]

The evidence thus supports the view that Twain, after stopping work upon "Eseldorf" in the fall of 1899 with the intention not of continuing it but of rewriting from the beginning, found by the summer of 1900 that imperialism had given him new subject matter and a new impulse to go on with the tale.[164]

His own circumstances in the summer of 1900 were right for sustained work at composition. On June 17 the New York *World* printed a cabled report describing him as "steadily working on his new book during his stay in London, living very quietly and keeping away from society so as not to be interrupted in his writing."[165] It was about two weeks thereafter, early in July, that he moved to Dollis Hill House, London, which was to be his home until his return to the United States in October, 1900. There he found even better conditions for writing, for Dollis was a secluded, peaceful place; he wrote to Twichell that he was "working & deep in the luxury of it."[166] By the end of July, he seems to have been far along in writing "Eseldorf," which must have been the manuscript to which he referred in a letter to Richard W. Gilder of July 31, 1900. He reported himself "25,000 words deep" in the writing of a story which he had, he thought, begun a good while before in Vienna; he also stated his intention of finishing it before turning to any other writing.[167] The phrase "25,000 words deep" could very well mean the amount of manuscript he had turned out during his latest, still sustained working period, rather than the total wordage of that and his earlier spurts. This larger total would then be the sum of the 29,500 words he had probably written by October, 1899, and the other 25,000—or 54,500 words. He would then, if these figures could be taken as accurate, have been within some five hundred words, or about four pages, of the end of the 423-page "Eseldorf" version, which has about 55,000 words. (These calculations are based upon word counts indicating an average of 130 words per page of the "Eseldorf" holograph.) Actually, as will be seen in a moment, he could not have been quite that far until the third week of August, 1900. But in view of his habit of overestimating his output (and in this case he was speaking in round figures and not necessarily trying to be precise), a somewhat reduced total is a more probable one. If he had written 22,500 words by the end of July, 1900, "Eseldorf" would then have totaled some 52,000 words and he would have reached approximately page 399. He could not at that time have written any further: beginning on page 399 and continuing through page 403, he made direct references to the assassination of King Humbert of Italy, which had occurred on July 29, 1900, and to certain related events which took place during the following three weeks. In particular, he commented upon an action taken by the Vatican on August 18, condemning (after having previously sanctioned) a prayer composed by the widowed Queen Margherita for her late husband the King, who had been excommunicated. This action was reported in the London *Times* of August 20; Twain, who regularly read the *Times,* would probably have known of the matter by that date. That he devoted some considerable amount of wordage to it suggests that he was writing while the incident was fresh in his mind. Moreover, the manner in which it was brought into the story indicates, in itself, a strictly contemporary reference: "A newspaper flashed into his [Satan's] hand,"[168] Theodor reports.

At this point Satan makes some pointed remarks about papal vacillation and the doctrine of infallibility, and he criticizes mankind for not seeing the humorous aspects of the cancellation of Queen Margherita's prayer. It is this incident to which Mark Twain is referring in the often-quoted passage, shorn of its particular application, which Paine and Duneka retained in editing *The Mysterious Stranger:*

> This multitude see the comic side of a thousand low-grade and trivial things—broad incongruities, mainly; grotesqueries, absurdities, evokers of the horse-laugh. The ten thousand high-grade comicalities which exist in the world are sealed from their dull vision.[169]

It seems likely that Mark Twain wrote this passage on or soon after August 20, and that he also wrote the remaining twenty pages of "Eseldorf" at that time. After relating an incident concerning a magic, many-fruited tree and the punishments inflicted by Satan upon its greedy owner, Twain continued for a few pages, not used in the published text, giving an account of Satan's performance of some conjuring tricks. Again, it seems, he had run out of plot. He may have been led into carrying the story beyond his intended conclusion (the outcome of the trial, presented on pages first numbered 84-93) by a desire to speak his mind about the condemnation of the Queen's prayer. Once he had expressed himself on that matter, he apparently had nothing to fall back upon except Satan's magic-tricks. He probably reached this point, thereby doing his last work upon "Eseldorf," some time late in August, 1900.

The evidence of the materials agrees with these findings. He had and used for other holographic manuscripts produced at Dollis Hill the two kinds of paper that he used for all of "Eseldorf" following page 85 (except, of course, pages 377-386). His "Letter to Times on Missionaries in China," for example, matches in its materials the greater part of "Eseldorf" (pages 86-376, 387-392);

not only the paper but the ink and the handwriting are, or appear to be, the same.[170] Likewise, his article "Dollis Hill House, London, 1900" as closely matches the concluding part (pages 393-423) that is on the ochre paper of slightly smaller size.[171]

When interviewed before and after his return to the United States in mid-October, 1900, he offered some comments which must have been in reference to his lately suspended work upon "Eseldorf." Before he left London, he reported, "I have a book half finished, but when the other half will be done the Lord only knows."[172] Upon reaching New York on October 15, he said more revealingly,

> I rewrote one of my books three times, and each time it was a different book. I had filled in, and filled in, until the original book wasn't there. It had evaporated through the blanks, and I had an entirely new book. I shall write my story, and then lay the scene where I want it, and, if necessary, change other things to suit the places.
>
> I shall very probably write a story with the scene laid in this country, or I shall place the scene of one of my present uncompleted stories here. This can be done rather handily, after the whole story is written.[173]

By this time he had, of course, made three attempts at writing the story of a young Satan: the first stint of work upon "Eseldorf" (including the "pre-Eseldorf" draft as well); the "Hannibal" version; and the revised and extended "Eseldorf" version. And, starting with the "pre-Eseldorf" beginning, he had first laid the scene in America, then had relocated it in Austria, then had brought it back to America (in writing "Hannibal"), and then had (in continuing "Eseldorf") returned it to Austria. He had indeed been changing scenes as readily as his reported comments would indicate. And it seems likely that he was then contemplating shifting the locale of "Eseldorf," one of his "present uncompleted stories," still another time.

Of particular interest is one further remark that he made when asked if he would "have any more like *Huckleberry Finn* and *Tom Sawyer*": "Yes, I shall have to do something of that kind, I suppose. But one can't talk about an unwritten book. It may grow into quite a different thing."[174] Some evidence may, just possibly, show that this intended Tom-and-Huck story was to be another version of *The Mysterious Stranger*—once again placed in an American setting. Some notebook entries, beginning in January, 1902, and continuing to July of that year, present ideas for a story to be called "Fifty Years Later."[175] The tale was to feature Hannibal characters, including Tom and Huck, first in their youth and then after half a century. And, in the margins of the original typescript copy of "Eseldorf," beside the part which tells of Satan's bringing down storm and fire upon the little people he has created,[176] there are these penciled notations in Twain's hand:

> Boys privately rescue them—2 or 3—& keep them for years,—Their lifetime is a 12th of ours—they raise families, have funerals, &c, they are invisible to all but the boys—they have tragedies & conflagrations & love passages & murders[.]
> Now—50 years later?—They are a very numerous [sic], & are two nations, divided by a ridge, & have wars of succession, & famous heroes, & crazy religions, & 2 languages.[177]

On the following page, after the sentence in the typescript which speaks of "not one of the five hundred poor creatures escaping," he noted, "Except a group found later."[178] He was evidently thinking of carrying on the story by enlarging and developing what is probably its most novel and most dramatic episode. The afterthought that provided for such a continuation, the idea of having the boys "privately rescue" a "group found later," is an interesting parallel of the note he had made at a crucial time in the writing of *Huckleberry Finn:* "Back a little, *change*—raft only crippled by steamer."[179] It appears that this improvisation that saved Huck's raft also saved Mark Twain's story by keeping the action on the Mississippi and in the river towns, where the author was imaginatively most at home and most in control of his material.[180] And it is at least possible that the rescuing of the diminutive race in *The Mysterious Stranger* might have taken that story in a direction which would have saved it from much of the moralistic exposition that filled the middle portion of the tale as he actually wrote it. By focusing upon the situation of the boys and their dependent race of manikins, he might have succeeded in projecting the human situation and man's moral involvement in a more appealing and convincing way than that of Satan's didacticism. His notes, and especially the phrase, "Now—50 years later?" seem to show that he considered adapting "Eseldorf" or at least some of it for the new story of Tom and Huck. He may have gone on to write a substantial part of such a story, though no such manuscript appears to have survived. In his dictation of August 30, 1906, he said that he had carried a story of Huck and Tom and Jim "as far as thirty-eight thousand words four years ago, then destroyed it. . . ."[181] And Paine has recorded that in October, 1902, Twain worked upon a story in which Huck and Tom were to appear first as boys and then as old men.[182]

Paine's designation of October as the time of composition may be too late. When interviewed early in September, 1902, Twain reportedly said: "I am not doing much writing, but up to the 11th of August I was busily engaged upon the novel that isn't finished yet, though I've been at it for four years. It's to be a fantastic book."[183] He had begun "Eseldorf" about four and one-half years previously and had worked on various drafts of young Satan's story during the following period; he could well have considered that he had "been at it for four years." And a tale in which Huck and Tom would consort with a boy-angel and would also become, in effect, deities watching over a Lilliputian race they had "saved" would have been "a fantastic book." It may have been "Fifty Years Later" that he dropped upon the 11th of August. And this may have been the work from which he read to Howells, who later recalled that during the summer of 1902 his friend had read

> the first chapters of an admirable story. The scene was laid in a Missouri town, and the characters such as he had known in boyhood; but often as I tried to make him own it, he denied having written any such story; it is possible that I dreamed it, but I hope the MS. will yet be found.[184]

If this was the manuscript that Twain destroyed, it will not, of course, be found, and its possible relation to *The Mysterious Stranger* will remain a matter for conjecture.

Whether the draft that he may then have been writing was recognizably another version of *The Mysterious Stranger* or not is uncertain. It does, however, seem clear that "Fifty Years Later," with its new plot-ideas, would have been a story quite different from "Eseldorf." And there is no evidence of any further work on the latter manuscript after Twain's return to the United States in October, 1900. Indeed, there is no more of that version to be accounted for; there is, to be sure, the six-page fragment which Paine added to "Eseldorf" as a conclusion for *The Mysterious Stranger,* but it was written as a part of the only version that remains to be considered—the "Print Shop" manuscript.[185]

5

"*P*RINT SHOP" *IS DEFINITELY* the version that Mark Twain wrote last. There is evidence that it could not, before the late fall of 1902, have been carried beyond the first two chapters; that the greater part of it was written in Florence in 1904; that the "dream-ending" used to complete the published story was written for this version—almost certainly in 1904—and set aside for later use; that all but one chapter had been written by the summer of 1905; and that the last-written chapter, comprising his final work upon any draft of *The Mysterious Stranger,* was not composed until 1908.

In this latest form of the story he combined some elements of both the "Eseldorf" and the "Hannibal" drafts and added to them much new material. Once again, after having perhaps most recently tried the story with an American background, he laid the scene in Austria. He began with the "Eseldorf" setting, adapting the first chapter of that version to make it serve as a beginning for "Print Shop." He added to the description of the village another castle, one neglected and mouldering. For this description he probably used recollections of his great house at Hartford, in which the Clemens family had spent their happier years; the place had remained closed after Susy's death there in 1896, for he and his wife could not bear living there afterward. He sold the house in the spring of 1903.[186] Thus, at about the time that he may have conceived the "Print Shop" setting, his own "castle" had a new master. And in the story the mouldering edifice is in the possession of a Master Stein,[187] who has set up in it one of the country's first print shops.

Mark Twain introduced this second castle immediately following the "borrowed" first chapter of "Eseldorf."[188] He also made revisions in the first chapter further to distinguish the original castle as "Rosenfeld," the property of a prince bearing that name.[189] The typescript of this first chapter followed these revisions and was actually the initial chapter of the typescript of "Print Shop,"[190] being in continuity with it but not with the following part of the typescript of "Eseldorf," with which it is presently placed in the Mark Twain Papers. Paine, in editing, deleted Twain's references to "Rosenfeld" and used the first chapter of the "Print Shop" typescript along with the "Eseldorf" typescript (the first chapter that was typed in continuity with the latter seems not to have survived) as, apparently, the printer's text for the published story.

Evidently Twain carried over from "Hannibal" the idea of introducing print-shop material that he had conceived before abandoning that draft. Also, he gave to the mysterious stranger of this version the same number-name that he used in "Hannibal": "44." In the story, "44," in the guise of a penniless young stranger, comes to the castle in search of work and is favored by the kindly Master Stein but persecuted by the latter's wife and step-daughter, as well as by most of the print-shop workers. The wife at first insists that "44" must sleep in the cellar (significantly, the first item in Twain's working notes for the beginning of "Print Shop" refers to a deposed king who is kept in a cellar). However, the Master gives him better quarters and also insists upon making him an apprentice. Mark Twain no doubt based these episodes upon his own first experiences as an apprentice to the printing trade in Hannibal, when he was in his twelfth year. As Paine has recorded, in the establishment of Joseph P. Ament, owner and editor of the Missouri *Courier,* the "apprentices ate in the kitchen at first, served by the old slave-cook and her handsome mulatto daughter; but those printer's 'devils' made it so lively there that in due time they were promoted to the family table"; however, "when food was scarce even an angel—a young printer angel—could hardly resist slipping down the cellar stairs at night for raw potatoes, onions, and apples which they carried into the office, where the boys slept on a pallet on the floor."[191]

August Feldner, the narrator of "Print Shop" and one of the shop workers, also befriends "44." The other workers, who become disgruntled when the master makes the stranger an apprentice, go on strike, refusing to get out the order of Bibles he has contracted to produce. But "44," who already has privately displayed to August his ability to do miracles, contrives to keep the work going by bringing in doubles—"duplicates"—of the striking printers. The duplicates are at first ghostly and invisible, but "44" presently materializes them, to the astonishment and confusion of all. He also performs various other incredible feats, letting an old magician take credit for them. (The "mysterious stranger" of "Print Shop" is just that: whereas the "44" of "Hannibal" reveals that he is Satan, Jr., this one guards the secret of his identity.) He then goes out of his way to stir up resentment and make enemies for himself (for no apparent reason); after finally being burned at the stake, he appears again, alive and unchanged. At this point, the plot shifts abruptly. Love-complications are introduced, as well as other problems resulting from the splitting of several characters into multiple selves—waking self, dream self, and immortal spirit. It has already been noted that he had explored this idea of multiple selves some years earlier, in an extended notebook entry of January 7, 1897. With the help of "44," August discovers hitherto unused powers within himself; he enjoys a new independence of time and space, roams at will throughout the universe, and seems to be coming close to supplanting "44" in such a role in the story. However, "44," still the master illusion-maker, thereafter presents a pageant-in-reverse, turning back the clocks and making history roll backward. Then, for a final grand review, he summons a spectral procession of the illustrious dead; just at the last, he waves away the vision he has conjured, and he and August stand alone in a vacant and silent world.

The procession of the dead is presented in the separately paginated fragment of eight pages which is a part of "Print Shop"; the foregoing part of the above summary refers to pages 23-587 of that manuscript. To this summary there might have been added the incidents of the other fragment of six pages, used as the conclusion of *The Mysterious Stranger;* it will be shown later that this conclusion, as Twain wrote it, does logically follow the eight-page fragment.

There appears to be no way to identify with certainty the time when Twain appropriated the first chapter of "Eseldorf" for a start upon this "Print Shop" story. Such a borrowing would presumably have been possible at any time after he had written that chapter late in 1897, but it is not at all likely that it occurred until he had abandoned "Eseldorf" (as it appears, in fact, that he did) and had come to think of it as material to draw upon in shaping another draft. He would not have used such a beginning for a "Tom and Huck" version of *The Mysterious Stranger* (if there was one), for he would not have needed the Austrian setting. About all that can be said is that the borrowing must have been done after he had left Dollis Hill, where he had been at work upon "Eseldorf," and thus after his return to America in the fall of 1900. It is also hard to date the brief second chapter of "Print Shop," which describes the previously mentioned castle and presents a cast of characters. But it is possible to establish the earliest time when the next chapter could have been composed. Six pages of further working notes, which were followed quite closely in the writing of the third chapter and some later ones, are in the holograph of Isabel V. Lyon.[192] And it seems that Miss Lyon did not become his secretary until the fall of 1902. The available records indicate that she had assumed her position by mid-November of that year, but there is no indication of her presence before that time.[193] The inference is that "Print Shop" was not, until at least as late as November, 1902, carried beyond the first two chapters. This deduction fits in well with the other evidence, which shows that the greater part of the manuscript was not written until 1904, after Mark Twain settled in Florence.

That he worked upon the story at Florence may readily be established by looking ahead for a moment to the time of his stay at Dublin, New Hampshire, in the summer of 1905. During most of that June he had been writing "3,000 Years Among the Microbes,"[194] but he had discontinued work upon that story a few days before the end of the month. On June 29 he wrote to his daughter Clara:

> I have spent the day reading the book I wrote in Florence. I destroyed 125 pages of it, & expect to go over it again tomorrow & destroy 25 more. Then I think I will take hold of it & finish it, dropping the microbe book meantime.[195]

And, on page 432 of "Print Shop," a note at the bottom in the Clemens holograph reads, "June 30/05 Burned the rest (30,000 words) of the book this morning[:] too diffusive." It is clear that this manuscript, which he went over on the following day, destroying pages as he had said he would do, is the one identified as the book written in Florence.

He had taken his family to Florence late in 1903, in the hope that the climate would benefit his wife, Olivia Langdon Clemens, who was then in what proved to be her last illness.[196] After taking residence there in Villa di Quarto, he occupied himself with the writing of a number of short pieces for magazines. Then, in January, 1904, having completed this task-work, he was ready for a more private and more serious kind of composition. He wrote to Twichell on January 7, 1904, that he expected to spend the rest of the year "on a couple of long books (half-completed ones)," adding, "No more magazine-work hanging over my head."[197] To Howells he reported, on January 16, "I expect to put in some of my afternoons on one or the other of my long stories, & by & by get both of them finished, but there is no hurry."[198]

In both of these letters he spoke of a continuation of one or two long stories already started. He was probably speaking of "Which Was Which?"[199] and "Print Shop," which are the two longest manuscripts of the Despair Group—and of any of the stories attempted after the completion of *Following the Equator* in 1897. The paper and ink of "Which Was Which?" do not, however, match those that he was using at Florence, and it is likely that he continued, at this time, only one long story, "Print Shop." That his work upon it was, in fact, a continuation and not a beginning is confirmed by both internal and external evidence.

What this evidence indicates is that Mark Twain probably wrote to about page 110 before going to Florence, and that it was at this point that he again took up the story. At page 110 he had reached the end of the seventh chapter and had concluded the account of the mysterious stranger's first day at the shop. But there are, in the pages that follow this comparatively well-unified section of the manuscript, several signs of a possible discontinuity in the composition. On page 116 he made his first reference to a new character, a drifting, nonchalant printer called "Doangivadam," whom he brought in—seemingly on the spur of the moment—as a champion for the mistreated "44" and the deserving Master Stein. And at page 119, after having called the shop-foreman (and chief persecutor of "44") "Blume" in the preceding part, he began to call him "Katzenyammer," adding a note to Jean Clemens, who was his typist, instructing her to go back and change the name from the beginning. What may be especially significant about this change is that the name "Katzenyammer" was used in "The $30,000 Bequest," a story he had written at Florence some time before that letter of January 7, 1904, in which he had spoken of being finished with such magazine writing.[200] In that story, he used this name as one that would serve to characterize a windy, self-important nobody. It is not unlikely that, in returning soon thereafter to his work upon "Print Shop," he found this name suited to the braggart and bully, Hans Blume, and made the change accordingly. At the same time he may have been trying to revive his plot. A new line of action is announced on page 129, in what sounds like a determined effort to get the story moving again, as well as a possible reference to his own situation in the trying period of his wife's illness: he wrote that August, hoping to avert the threatened strike of the printers, had gotten the idea "to cheer up, on our side, and stop despairing & get down to work—bring to our help every supernatural force that could be had for love or money." All of these considerations suggest that he probably resumed work upon the story at about page 110 and that he had written the preceding pages before coming to Florence. It has already been shown that he could not have begun the third chapter any earlier than November, 1902. He may have written the first 110 pages or so while at Riverdale, New York, in the spring of 1903;[201] or he may have done so at Quarry Farm, Elmira, where he stayed that fall before going abroad.[202]

Some help in dating his further work upon "Print Shop" at Florence is afforded by the evidence of his materials. The paper of pages 23-432 is that of the cheap, glossy, pearl-gray tablet stock, size 5⅝″ by 9″, which Twain began to use shortly after his return to America in 1900 and which he used rather regularly from 1902 through 1904. Thus, the part of the manuscript that is on this paper is that which follows the initial, "borrowed" chapter of "Eseldorf" (pages 1-22), through to the point at which he took up the story again in 1905 (page 433). More revealing than these facts about the paper, however, are those concerning the inks used in "Print Shop." Here are the variations:

Pages		*Ink*
1-22	("Eseldorf" Chapter I)	black
23-171		dark blue

172-214		vivid light blue
215-432		purplish blue
433-587		black
1-8	(fragment)	black
1-6	(fragment)	purplish blue[203]

First, it seems possible, by comparing the inks here found with those appearing in some of his other holographic writings, to determine approximately when he could have been writing certain parts of the story during the stay at Florence. The dark blue ink of pages 23-171, for example, matches that used in "Italian Without A Master," which he wrote before the end of 1903.[204] The vivid light blue ink was used in a letter of February 27, 1904.[205] And, most interestingly, in "The Honest Rebel"[206] he switched when half-way through the manuscript from the dark blue ink (pages 1-40) to the purplish blue (pages 41-81). Three more pages in the dark blue ink, originally written as an introduction and numbered 1-3 but then converted to an epilogue and re-paginated 82-84, conclude with his signature and date: "Mark Twain[,] Villa di Quarto, Florence, January, 1904." An added note states that the essay was sent to *Harper's* on February 19, 1904. He had, then, been using the dark blue ink in January but had changed to the purplish blue by February 19, or rather before that time (it would have required at least several days for the writing of pages 41-81 and the subsequent typing of the manuscript before mailing). As it happens, "The Honest Rebel" appears to represent both his latest use of the dark blue and his earliest use of the purplish blue ink while in Florence. These findings, when related to the facts of his use of inks in "Print Shop," suggest that in the latter story he may have gotten as far at page 171, on which is found the last of the dark blue, by mid-February if not sooner; that he may have written pages 172-214 in the light blue in February—perhaps near the end of that month; and that he wrote pages 215-432 in the purplish blue ink between the latter part of February and the end of his period of residence at Florence. It may be added that this purplish blue shade also appears in the notebook he kept at Florence, beginning with an entry of April 3 and continuing until June 20, 1904, when he left Florence; thereafter the entries are in black ink and the purplish blue color does not appear any more.[207] The use of this latter color of ink seems to have occurred only during the last four months of his stay at Villa di Quarto, thus fixing the time of composition of the middle part (pages 215-432) of "Print Shop" and of the previously-mentioned six-page fragment which furnished a final chapter for *The Mysterious Stranger*.[208]

This fragment, in which the story arrives at the solipsistic conclusion, *"Life itself is only a vision, a dream,"*[209] is paginated 1-6 and is headed on the first page, "Conclusion of the book." It has been noted that the materials of "Eseldorf" do not at all match those of this ending. The latter is, however, matched exactly by pages 215-432 of "Print Shop"—in the paper, the handwriting, the fineness of the pen-point, and, most significantly, the purplish blue ink. This evidence reveals that Mark Twain almost certainly wrote the "dream-ending" at Florence, and that he wrote it as an anticipated conclusion, while he was more or less in the middle of composition of the story. Such an anticipation was probably no unique event in his composition. The short chapter that he wrote as the ending for *Christian Science* is a similar fragment, headed "Conclusion" and separately paginated 1-7; this unit presumably was not written in sequence with the part just preceding, and it could easily have been drafted before that part had been written.[210]

The characters named in the solipsistic conclusion, as written by Twain, are those of the "Print Shop" version. The manuscript shows the editorial changes that were made by Paine to make the fragment fit "Eseldorf": where the names "44" and "August" occur, these have been deleted and "Satan" and "Theodor" inserted. The last paragraph of Chapter X and the first paragraph of the concluding Chapter XI of *The Mysterious Stranger* were also supplied as editorial additions to make the "Print Shop" fragment serve for the completion of "Eseldorf."[211] By such editorial carpentry, the ending that Twain had intended for his latest form of *The Mysterious Stranger* was joined to a form of it that he had almost certainly not worked upon since the summer of 1900.

"Print Shop" is the version that Mark Twain himself called "The Mysterious Stranger." His title for "Eseldorf" had been "The Chronicle of Young Satan." It was probably when he took the first chapter of "Eseldorf" to use as the beginning of "Print Shop" that he struck out the original title and wrote "The Mysterious Stranger." On page 24 of "Print Shop," he at first wrote "The Mysterious Stranger" and added, "Put in (Description of the region from the 'Young Satan')."[212]

It is of interest to determine as exactly as possible the time of the composition of the dream-ending. The evidence of the materials indicates that it was probably no earlier than February and clearly before the departure from Florence on June 20, 1904. And another piece of evidence suggests that it was quite possibly written some time near the end of the stay at Florence, during the ordeal of those last weeks or days before the death of Olivia. Before the middle of May, he had come to expect the worst, even when there appeared to be some promise of a recovery. On May 12 he wrote to Richard W. Gilder:

> For two entire days, now, we have not been anxious about Mrs. Clemens (unberufen). After 20 months of bed-ridden solitude and bodily misery she all of a sudden ceases to be a pallid shrunken shadow, and looks bright and young and pretty. She remains what she always was, the most wonderful creature of fortitude, patience, endurance and recuperative power that ever was. But ah, dear, it won't last; this fiendish malady will play new treacheries upon her, and I shall go back to my prayers again—unutterable from any pulpit!

The following morning, he added this postscript:

> May 13 10 A.M. I have just paid one of my pair of permitted 2 minutes visits per day to the sick room. And found what I have learned to expect —retrogression, and that pathetic something in the eye which betrays the secret of a waning hope.[213]

He had been, on May 9, already in the mood and situation that might have led him to write the conclusion when, having waited in vain for the chance of a two-minute visit in the sickroom (his wife had had a bad night and could stand no excitement), he wrote to Muriel Pears that he would give up his vigil and take himself "to the work which sweeps this world away, & puts me in one which no one has visited but me—nor will, for this book is not being written for print. . . ."[214] If he then went to his work upon "Print Shop," as would seem to be the case, he would have done so at a moment just after he had been associating it with the solipsistic idea that is the dominating concept of that chapter in which it is revealed, *"Nothing exists save empty space— and you!"*[215]

He must, of course, have often been in about the same mood during those days when the end was approaching. The foregoing considerations are no proof that he wrote that chapter on May 9. But they do show that he was mentally and emotionally disposed toward writing it during the period when the other evidence shows that it must have been written, and they suggest that the latter part of that period would have been an especially likely time for such composition.

At least one further consideration suggests that he wrote the dream ending at about the time that death took away the wife he had so deeply loved. The transitional paragraph which begins the final chapter in the published text was supplied by Paine as an editorial insertion and is not to be found in the holograph. As Twain wrote it, the chapter begins with August's question to "44";

> "And you are going away, and will not come back any more?
> "Yes," he said. "We have comraded long together, and it has been pleasant—pleasant for both; but I must go now, and we shall not see each other any more.216

The opening question is, save for the style of its utterance, the same one that had lingered in Mark Twain's thoughts as a kind of sorrowful refrain after the death of Susy. At that time, he had written:

> She took such interest in all my work—and I miss her so—and half the incentive is gone.
> Those words touched her so: "And will you no come back again."217

And he had jotted down some lines of a lament in which he asked the sorrowful question repeatedly.218 The words that had so touched Susy were a part of a dramatization of Twain's *Pudd'nhead Wilson,* which she had seen on the stage. It may be significant that he spoke of Susy as the one who had furnished *half* the incentive for his literary work; the implication, surely, is that his wife furnished the other half. And, although he almost certainly did not think of Mrs. Clemens as the original of "44," he could easily have thought of her at the time of her death as the one whose spirit and force had sustained him and inspired his art; he could thereby have related his personal loss to his narrator's loss of the companionship of the mysterious stranger.

Nevertheless, it appears likely that Mark Twain regarded this chapter more as a literary solution than as a personal one. That he titled it "Conclusion of the Book" shows, in fact, that it was explicitly a *story-solution*. And on the back cover of a tablet of the kind that he was using at Florence, and in the purplish blue ink in which the dream ending is written, he had noted a character-description—that of a man who looked intelligent and calm and sane but who had as his "foible" the notion that existence was a dream; that God and the whole of creation were a dream; that he was the only one in the universe; that he was, himself, only a foolish thought roaming endlessly in the void.[219] This note, of course, very closely parallels the revelation that comes at the end of *The Mysterious Stranger:*

> "It is true, that which I have revealed to you; there is no God, no universe, no human race, no earthly life, no heaven, no hell. Nothing exists but you. And you are but a *thought*—a vagrant thought, a useless thought, a homeless thought, wandering forlorn among the empty eternities!"

Those are the parting words of Satan (or "44"), and the tale is then concluded with the narrator's statement: "He vanished, and left me appalled; for I knew, and realized, that all he had said was true."[220] Twain's note may indicate that, unlike his narrator, he did not necessarily accept this solipsistic view as his own; that he perhaps considered that the "life-is-only-a-dream" idea betokened a certain frailty or slight weakness on the part of anyone who would take it altogether seriously.

Mark Twain, it should be noted, was familiar with the idea that life is only a dream long before the time of his writing this conclusion; any assumption that he arrived at it through the writing of any version of *The Mysterious Stranger* is, in fact, untenable. He was writing articles about Christian Science as early as the spring of 1898;[221] he had for that purpose studied its doctrines and would have been well acquainted with the belief that "Mortal existence is a dream; mortal existence has no real entity,"[222] as stated by Mary Baker Eddy in *Science and Health*. Indeed, the sheet of working notes for beginning "Eseldorf," presented in an earlier chapter, has on the reverse side in Twain's hand a passage copied from *Science and Health:* "Finite belief can never do justice to Truth in any direction. It limits all things and would compress Mind, which is infinite, beneath a skull-bone."[223] A vertical pencil-mark has been struck through this material, which he probably canceled at the time that he made (in pencil) the notes on the other side. His knowledge of the doctrines of Christian Science evidently antedated his initial work upon "Eseldorf." It is interesting to find Christian Science material thus juxtaposed to his notes for that early version of the story. And it will be seen in the next chapter that he used such material in his latest version, "Print Shop."

6

AFTER SPENDING A LONELY winter in New York, Mark Twain took residence at Dublin, New Hampshire, for the summer of 1905. He wrote regularly during his stay, which was to be the time of his last major outburst of creativity. He reached Dublin on May 20 and soon began writing the story which he called "3,000 Years Among the Microbes,"[224] presenting a view of the human situation that had been in his thoughts for many years. On August 12, 1884, he had noted, "I think we are only the microscopic trichina concealed in the blood of some vast creature's veins, and it is that vast creature whom God concerns Himself about and not us."[225] Much the same concept may be found in a passage that he wrote some twelve years later in *Following the Equator:*

> In Sydney I had a large dream. . . . I dreamed that the visible universe is the physical person of God; that the vast worlds that we see twinkling millions of miles apart in the fields of space are the blood-corpuscles in His veins; and that we and the other creatures are the microbes that charge with multitudinous life the corpuscles.[226]

It has been shown that some of his notes of September and October, 1897, seem to refer to the "microbe story," for which he had probably done some planning not long after the writing of *Following the Equator.* At Dublin, after an interval of more than seven years, he finally got the story under way. It purports to be "The Autobiography of a Microbe, Who, In a Former Existence, Had Been a Man—His Present Habitat Being the Organism of a Tramp, Blitzowski."[227] Twain's microbe narrator finds, after his transformation, that microbes are themselves infested by far smaller germs proportionately as minute as are microbes in comparison to people. But his fellow germs do not know that *they* are, in turn, inhabiting a creature that is correspondingly more vast:

> He did not suspect that he, also, was engaged in gnawing, torturing, defiling, rotting, and murdering a fellow-creature—he and all the swarming billions of his race. None of them suspects it. That is significant. It hints at the possibility that the procession of known and listed devourers is not complete. It suggests the possibility, and substantially the certainty, that man is himself a microbe, and his globe a blood-corpuscle drifting with its shining brethren of the Milky Way down a vein of the Master of all things, whose body, mayhap—glimpsed partwise from the earth by night, and receding and lost to view in the measureless remotenesses of space—is what men name the Universe.228

The narrator of "3,000 Years Among the Microbes" is another of Mark Twain's mysterious strangers. He comes into the subordinate world of the microbes from an existence as a being immensely superior in size and knowledge and power. And in his new life he retains some attributes of his previous one: his body, for example, keeps human time, giving him an incalculably long life span, or virtual immortality, in terms of little, short "microbe-years"—very much as is the case for Philip Traum, the sixteen-thousand-year-old angel boy, and also (presumably) for the mysterious strangers of "Hannibal" and "Print Shop."

Mark Twain carried the microbe story to about 40,000 words before putting it aside. On June 11, 1905, he wrote to Clara, his daughter, that by 2:45 p.m. on that day he had already done sixteen pages, although twelve would have been a full day's work. He added that he had reached page 240 in the manuscript, all of which he had written at Dublin since May 20.229 Within the next two weeks, he apparently wrote the remaining part of the 361-page draft,230 which he left incomplete. The story breaks off after the narrator has let it be seen that he himself is corrupt and contemptible, an exploiter of those who are inferior to him. On June 24 Twain wrote to Twichell that he had started his new book thirty-five days previously and had done thirty-three consecutive days of work upon it. The only interruption, he indicated, had come on June 5, the anniversary of Olivia's death, when he had done no work; he had then continued until June 23.231 A few days later, he was preparing to resume work upon "Print Shop."

To Clara he wrote the letter of June 29, mentioned previously, which deserves to be quoted again: "I have spent the day reading the book I wrote in Florence. I destroyed 125 pages of it, & expect to go over it again tomorrow & destroy 25 more. Then I think I will take hold of it & finish it, dropping the microbe book meantime."[232] On the following day he noted, on page 432 of the "Print Shop" manuscript, "June 30/05 Burned the rest (30,000 words) of the book this morning[:] too diffusive."[233]

The materials offer confirmation that pages 433-587, comprising all of the remaining part except one additional chapter, were written in 1905. These pages are of the white, non-glossy paper and are written in the black ink that he used commonly in 1905. Moreover, the writing on these pages has the sidewise placement (lines written across the length, rather than the width, of the paper) that he employed with curious consistency in 1905 but probably at no other time.[234] Internal evidence also confirms the fact of composition at this time. On page 535 Twain pinned a newspaper clipping which he represented in the story as having been materialized from the future by the magic of "44." "Date, June 27, four hundred & thirteen years hence,"[235] the latter explains. The clipping quotes a special request to her church members by Mary Baker Eddy, dated June 27, 1905; it is likely that he introduced it into "Print Shop" a few days later, after he had resumed work on the story on June 30 and had written an additional 103 pages.

As the bringing in of this topical material might suggest, he was having his usual trouble in finding a plot-line. But he seems to have written exuberantly at this time, and rapidly. And it is very probable that he wrote pages 433-587, comprising about 18,600 words, before mid-July, by which time he had already turned to other writing. His letter of July 16 to F. A. Duneka reveals that he had by then completed "Eve's Diary," much of which he had written during the previous winter, and had also revised "Adam's Diary" by inserting "5 MS pages of new matter (650 words)."[236] On the same day, July 16, he wrote to Clara that Duneka had lately visited him and had wanted him to get "Eve's Diary" ready for the Christmas issue of *Harper's*, and that he had then finished it in three days.[237] It thus appears that he discontinued the composition of "Print Shop" in order to do the requested magazine work.

Mark Twain's dictation of July 17, 1906, explains what happened at the time of this abrupt change. He recalled the time that Duneka had visited him at Dublin in the summer of 1905 and had read one of his unfinished stories, which had its scene laid in the Middle Ages. Upon finding in it a Catholic priest much given to profanity and drunkenness, he had shuddered; he had "wanted the priest reformed or left out."[238] Twain added that he was an excellent editor when his religion (Duneka was a Roman Catholic) didn't get in the way of his literary work. In starting to read "Print Shop," Duneka would at once have found in the borrowed Chapter I of "Eseldorf" the hostile description of Father Adolf (originally Lueger) that has already been noted. It is likely that he read the manuscript while Twain was working on it, and that his unfavorable opinion squelched the creative exuberance that might otherwise have carried the story to its conclusion at that time.

In still another letter of July 16, 1905, he wrote that he had turned out well over 100,000 words at Dublin and that his mill was still grinding.[239] But there is no indication that he did any further work upon "Print Shop" during the rest of the summer. In fact, it can be said that there is no evidence that, save for one additional chapter which will be considered later, he ever did any more writing of any version of *The Mysterious Stranger*.

On August 3, 1905, he wrote to Clara that he was happy to hear that she planned to be with him at 21 Fifth Avenue, New York, when he returned in the fall. After speaking fancifully of her coming there in her moccasins, feathers, and war-paint to take over the running of the household, he added, parenthetically, that he had broken his bow and burned his arrows.[240] His expression recalls Prospero's—and supposedly Shakespeare's—valedictory speech in *The Tempest*, renouncing the practice of his "so potent art":

> . . . I'll break my staff,
> Bury it certain fathoms in the earth,
> And deeper than did ever plummet sound
> I'll drown my book.[241]

It is not unlikely that Mark Twain had this passage in mind.

In a memorandum to Duneka, written on October 9, 1905, he reported that he had stopped working after writing the "first half" of "The Adventures of a Microbe" and of "The Mysterious

Stranger" and had put both tales away "for a finish next summer."
He realized that such a cessation of creative effort in midsummer
was a departure from a long-established habit: "Since I stopped
work I have had a two months' holiday. The summer has been
my working time for 35 years; to have a holiday in it (in America)
is new for me."[242] According to Twain's reckoning, his "two
months' holiday" must have been begun in the early part of
August, or about the time of his writing of what may be a valediction in the letter of August 3.

In the summer of 1906, he again stayed at Dublin; however, he
did very little writing. He spent many hours dictating chapters of
his *Autobiography* "to a stenographer, usually in the open air,
sitting in a comfortable rocker or pacing up and down the long
veranda that faced a vast expanse of wooded slope and lake and
distant blue mountains."[243] "The dictating goes lazily and pleas-
antly on,"[244] he wrote to Howells on June 17. In his dictation of
August 30, 1906, he spoke of books that he had left unfinished.
Of "The Adventures of a Microbe During Three Thousand Years—
by a Microbe," he stated, "It is half finished and will remain so."
He continued, "There is yet another—*The Mysterious Stranger*.
It is more than half finished. I would dearly like to finish it, and
it causes me a real pang to reflect that it is not to be." He was, he
said, "tired of the pen."[245]

On October 2, 1906, he wrote to Thomas Bailey Aldrich, Howells'
successor as editor of the *Atlantic,* that after having worked for
sixty-five years he was no longer concerned about wasting time.[246]
And in his dictation of November 8, 1906, he stated: "Not even
yet have I really written myself out. I have merely stopped writing
because dictating is pleasanter work"; he also commented, "I shall
never finish my five or six unfinished books, for the reason that by
forty years of slavery to the pen I have earned my freedom. I
detest the pen and wouldn't use it again to sign the death warrant
of my dearest enemy."[247]

Despite his assertion that he had not written himself out, it
appears that his creative powers had finally flagged. Although his
imagination was still active, he lacked the energy for the hard
work with the pen needed to embody his fancies in fiction. To
Clara he wrote on July 27, 1907, that he was glad to hear that she
was absorbed in the labors of her art (Clara Clemens was an
accomplished pianist and singer). He added that such a life was

like the one he had lived long ago with the pen; that no other kind of life could be compared to it; that only genius could live splendidly, regally, in the towered and pinnacled palaces, gilt and bejeweled, which were provided by those "splendid hellions," the genie-slaves of the master artist.[248] It may be supposed that Mark Twain would not have relinquished these powers had he still been able to wield them. In putting away his pen, he was resigning himself to a diminished existence.

During his last several years there were, to be sure, times when he enjoyed a brief return of the strength he needed for literary creation. Apparently it was at one of these times that he composed the chapter required to bring "Print Shop" to its previously written conclusion. In 1906, he had referred to the story as "more than half finished"; in reckoning the degree of completeness that the book had attained, he may have been thinking not so much of additional wordage as of integration and revision. At any rate, it seems that very late in his life he indicated to Paine that only a little writing would be necessary to conclude the story. According to Paine's latest account of the matter, Twain at his Stormfield home had on one occasion referred to *The Mysterious Stranger* as a work that he "could finish very easily, almost any time." Also, Paine related that he had found, several years later, "that amazing final chapter, of the best version, probably written . . . about the time of our conversation."[249] Here he was referring to the fragment that he used to complete "Eseldorf"—the conclusion for "Print Shop" that had been written in 1904 at Florence. Paine supposed that it had been written only after the reported conversation, which he thought had occurred in 1909. But it must be considered that his recollections as set down in his edition of the notebooks were not written until some thirty years after those events. There is evidence that Mark Twain actually wrote, while at Stormfield and probably in 1908, not that conclusion but the chapter of "Print Shop" in which "44" shows August Feldner the ghostly procession of the famous dead of all ages, then finally waves it all into oblivion, after which the two are left alone in "an empty & soundless world."[250]

The materials of this chapter are quite different from those of the rest of "Print Shop." The paper, of a light tan color and of good substance with a distinctive pattern of watermark lines, is a kind that Twain used for various manuscripts and letters which he wrote in 1908 and 1909. The handwriting is also clearly very late, having very much the same characteristics that may be observed in the sample of his writing of November 30, 1908, that has been reproduced by Paine in his *Biography*.[251] A manuscript which matches the chapter not only in the paper but also in the ink, the handwriting, and the fineness of pen-point is "On Sam Moffett," which he wrote in memory of his nephew, dating it August 16, 1908.[252] These facts might in themselves serve to establish the approximate time of composition of this remaining part of "Print Shop" and to show that it was written after the rest of the story and of course after the other versions of *The Mysterious Stranger*. But stronger evidence is to be found in a letter that Twain wrote to a Mrs. Hookway of Chicago, concerning children's theater programs (wherein the children staged their own plays under adult direction), in which he was at that time much interested. The letter is undated, but Paine, in publishing it, dated it September, 1908. Like the memorial statement, it fully matches the "Print Shop" chapter in paper, ink, pen-point, and handwriting. Furthermore its contents are such as to suggest that it and that chapter were perhaps written on the same day.

The letter begins with his statement that he had been "full of the spirit of work this morning, a rarity . . . lately." By work he would have meant composition. He had, he continued, been reading of the children's theater movement in Chicago. Reporting himself "stirred to [his] deepest deeps," he proceeded to give an enthusiastic account of the benefits which it was uniquely able to confer:

> It is much the most effective teacher of morals and promoter of good conduct that the ingenuity of man has yet devised, for the reason that its lessons are not taught wearily by book and by dreary homily, but by *visible and enthusing action;* and *they go straight to the heart,* which is the rightest of right places for them. Book morals often get no further than the intellect, if they even get that far on their *spectral and shadowy pilgrimage;* but when they travel from a Children's Theatre they do not stop permanently at that halfway house, but *go on home.*
>
> The children's theatre is the only teacher of morals and conduct and high ideals that never bores the pupil, but always leaves him sorry when the lesson is over. And as for history, no other teacher is for a moment comparable to it: no other can *make the dead heroes of the world rise up and shake the dust of the ages from their bones and live and move and breathe and speak and be real to the looker and listener;* no other can make the *study of the lives and times of the illustrious dead* a delight, a

splendid interest, a passion; and no other can *paint a history-lesson in colors that will stay, and stay, and never fade.*253

Italics have here been supplied to distinguish the parts of this letter which most closely parallel, in their phrasing or in their ideas, certain elements in the "Print Shop" chapter. For the benefit of young August, "44" provides a history pageant that is strikingly similar in its features and effects to what is, in the letter, claimed for the children's theater. Just as it is said that such a theater can "make the dead heroes of the world rise up and shake the dust of the ages from their bones and live," so does "44" quicken "his Assembly of the Dead. He summoned those forlorn wrecks from all the world & from all the epochs & ages," August relates, and soon it was possible to see "the spidery dim forms of thousands of skeletons marching." And, with the help of his mentor, August does in effect study the "lives and times of the illustrious dead": "44" names to him many of the passing skeletons who "had been distinguished in their day & had cut a figure in the world"; moreover, by his magic "each skeleton had a tab on him giving his name & date, & telling all about him, in brief." And it is shown that this history-pageant, like the children's theater, goes "straight to the heart" of the young person viewing it. August is touched by the pathetic sight of a young mother who had lost her child: "When I looked at her tab I saw it had happened five hundred thousand years ago! It seemed strange that it should still affect me, but I suppose such things never grow old, but remain always new." He had, in the words of the letter, seen a history lesson painted "in colors that will stay . . . and never fade." It is almost as if Twain had written the chapter of his story as an illustration of the generalizations presented in his letter to Mrs. Hookway. Or perhaps it was the other way around. In either case, the degree of parallelism that obtains between these two pieces of writing, together with the close agreement of their materials, suggests that both could easily have been written on the same day, and that the "spirit of work" which came to Mark Twain that morning at Stormfield was quite possibly devoted in part to the last-written chapter of "Print Shop" and the last work that he ever did upon the story which, in an earlier form, he had begun in Vienna almost eleven years before.254

This chapter, at the end of which much of reality fades away to leave August and "44" alone in "an empty & soundless world,"

could probably serve well enough as a conclusion for "Print Shop."
But it also brings the story to a point from which Twain's anticipated conclusion logically follows: in that "dream-ending," which
had been written in 1904, "44" then fades into nothingness and
only August remains, "a homeless thought, wandering forlorn
among the empty eternities."[255] In continuing "Print Shop" in
1905, Twain apparently began to lead the story toward this intended conclusion. It is in this part that August seems about to
take the place of "44" as one who wields unlimited powers of
mind. Actually, the one so privileged is his "dream-self," an entity
who leads his own life and, like "44," roves at will throughout time
and space. "Past & Future" are "all one thing to a dream-sprite."[256]
Moreover, like "44" he is contemptuous of human life as experi-
enced by the "waking-self": most things, he tells August, are
"above your dull Mortal Mind's reach."[257] (The term "Mortal
Mind" is one much used in Mary Baker Eddy's writings on Christian Science.) However, after being "materialized" by the magic
of "44," the dream-sprite finds himself bound by the limitations
of physical existence. He then begs "44" to release him (and it
must be considered that, in the terms of the story, it is August's
own unconscious mind that is asking to be freed):

> Oh, mighty one, you imprisoned me, you can set me free, & no other can.
> You have the power; you possess *all* the powers, all the forces that defy
> Nature. . . .258

In the final, solipsistic chapter, "44," who turns out to be a projection of August's creative imagination, does give the latter his
freedom by discovering to him the sovereignty of his own unconscious mind:

> I am but a dream—your dream, creature of your imagination. In a
> moment you will have realized this, then you will banish me from your
> visions and I shall dissolve into the nothingness out of which you made
> me. . . .
>   I am perishing already—I am failing—I am passing away. In a little
> while you will be alone in shoreless space, to wander its limitless solitudes
> without friend or comrade forever—for you will remain a *thought*, the
> only existent thought, and by your nature inextinguishable, indestructible.
> But I, your poor servant, have revealed you to yourself and set you free.259

The last quoted sentence shows "44" granting the release requested in the foregoing passage. It is probable that Mark Twain

had been writing with this ending in mind in 1905. And it is also likely that he still had it, as well as the rest of "Print Shop," in mind in 1908, when he did the additional writing necessary to bring the story through to the chapter that he had written in Florence and had titled "Conclusion of the book."[260]

7

THE FINDINGS OF THIS study are here summarized, showing the order and approximate times of composition of the existing
versions of *The Mysterious Stranger:*

"Pre-Eseldorf" pages (includ-ed in "Eseldorf" as pages 53, 56-72, 74)*	October, 1897
"Eseldorf," pages 1-52, 54-55, 73, 75-85, 377-386	November, 1897–January, 1898
"Hannibal"	November–December, 1898
"Eseldorf," continued	
Pages 86-228	May–October, 1899
Pages 229-376, 387-423	June–August, 1900
"Print Shop"	
Pages 23-110	November, 1902–October, 1903
Pages 111-432	January–June, 1904
Six-page fragment ("Con-clusion of the book")	February–June, 1904
Pages 433-587	June–July, 1905
Eight-page fragment ("add-ed" chapter)	September, 1908

These findings show that Mark Twain was intermittently engaged in writing the several manuscripts over a period of nearly

-----

* Page 58½, inserted by Mark Twain in the sequence of pages 56-72,
was not a part of the "pre-Eseldorf" draft.

eleven years. *The Mysterious Stranger* was the story that he most persistently worked on during this time; he returned to it repeatedly, almost as often changing the plot and the locale in his attempts to find the right form for the tale.

It is clear, however, that *The Mysterious Stranger* as published does not represent Mark Twain's intention. In view of the extensive editorial omissions and additions, the published text cannot even be regarded as his intended form of "Eseldorf." Furthermore, he abandoned that version after doing his last work upon it in 1900; thereafter he used the first chapter as the beginning of "Print Shop." He composed the latter story as the latest and also the longest of the versions, and the only one which he carried to a conclusion. Moreover, "Print Shop" is the manuscript that Twain himself called "The Mysterious Stranger." He so named it when he began writing it and so identified it when he did his last work upon it.[261]

It is also evident that the actual order of composition of the versions is very nearly the reverse of the one that was assumed by DeVoto, who supposed that Twain had written first "Hannibal," then "Print Shop," and finally "Eseldorf."[262] "Eseldorf" was actually written, not as the final draft of the story by which the author "saved himself in the end," but as the first of the existing versions; it was written during the years 1897-1900 and thus during the period that DeVoto believed had been a "time of desolation whose symbol he was not yet able to forge."[263]

The "dream ending" chapter, it is clear, was not intended for "Eseldorf," to which it was joined in the published version. Composed in 1904, some three and one-half years after Mark Twain had abandoned "Eseldorf," it was written as an anticipated conclusion for "Print Shop," while he was in the middle of his work on that version. It is not surprising, therefore, that E. S. Fussell has found in *The Mysterious Stranger* "striking contradictions" which "cannot easily be dismissed."[264]

It appears that much that has been supposed about *The Mysterious Stranger,* and indeed about Twain's later period, may have to be reconsidered. The theory that he "saved himself in the end" by writing the story that has been published (actually the "Eseldorf" version and the "Print Shop" conclusion) has been widely accepted as a basis for explaining what happened to him and to his literary work. The findings do not support that theory, and there seems to be a need for reappraisal and reinterpretation. It is hoped that this study of Mark Twain's writing of the several versions of *The Mysterious Stranger* will to some degree contribute toward a better understanding of the direction and tendency of his later writings.

Possibly it will be found that an important problem of his art during his later period was one of finding new material—a usual concern of the functioning literary artist but perhaps a crucial one for Mark Twain. The recollections of Hannibal which had served as the base of much of his writing had become temporally, geographically, and psychologically remote from the aging global traveler and unofficial ambassador to world capitals. Significantly, his attempts to use these remembrances in the story of little Satan did not succeed very well. It was when he made use of more recent experiences that the tale went forward strongly. Contemporary events in Austria in 1897 furnished an impetus for the beginning of "Eseldorf"; current military actions in China and in South Africa prompted him to continue that version in 1900 and to "dump" into it other topical material—the diatribe on "The Lowest Animal" which he had written at the time of the Cretan Revolt. News events that followed the death of King Humbert of Italy moved Twain to write the last part of "Eseldorf." And it has been seen that his very last work upon his latest version of *The Mysterious Stranger* was evidently prompted by recent news of a children's theater movement. These are but a few instances of his use of current events for story material in "Eseldorf" and "Print Shop"; he used little, if any, of such material when he attempted the "Hannibal" version.

He had long ago taken physical leave of Hannibal—in 1853, or roughly half a century before the writing of *The Mysterious Stranger*—and had made only a few brief return visits at long intervals thereafter. He had not maintained any really vital connection with the one place in the world most important to his art. The Hannibal memories, once so vivid and compelling, must have "thinned away and thinned away" like the disappearing Philip Traum, until many of them had become ghostlike in their vagueness, their insubstantiality. It is remarkable that Mark Twain should have been able to draw upon his diminishing supply as long as he did. That he tried so persistently to base his fiction upon such memories even when they had aged fifty years and had grown dim and stale suggests that he had perhaps never found any other sustaining basis for literary creation—that is, for his "serious" work of the more deeply and personally meaningful sort.

During much of his adult life he was an illustrious vagabond; once he left his home town, he never put down strong roots in any other locality. Even after his marriage to Olivia Langdon, he remained somewhat a drifter, and the periods of residence in the Hartford mansion might be considered extended sojourns of the Clemens family, who lived a semi-nomadic existence. One of the many paradoxes of Mark Twain's life is that he became a citizen of the world and was in a way at home everywhere, but that he was in a deeper sense homeless. And it seems likely that in the later years his life and consequently his art had become so nearly rootless that he had to depend upon the news handouts of the latest day and hour for literary sustenance.[265] If so, his problem was that of a maker with no adequate supply of material for making anything; it might even be said that his art required the unlimited powers of a creator who could make something out of nothing. It has been seen that these were, indeed, the powers claimed by Satan, the mysterious stranger:

> My mind creates! Do you get the force of that? Creates anything it desires—and in a moment. Creates without material. Creates fluids, solids, colors—anything, everything—out of the airy nothing which is called Thought.[266]

In the final chapter of *The Mysterious Stranger,* after revealing that he is himself a dream-creation of the narrator, Satan informs the latter, "I shall dissolve into the nothingness out of which you made me." His statement indicates that the teller of this tale enjoys a lordly independence of the physical world, of all material.

Pascal Covici, Jr., is no doubt right in feeling that in this concluding chapter "one can still sense . . . an integrated commitment to the artist's autonomy as maker."[267] It might be added that there is an insistence upon an autonomy so absolute as to deny that art must have access to nature, must nourish itself on reality, must have a matter as well as a form. The revealing remarks that Mark Twain made upon returning to America in 1900 deserve further consideration here. When asked if he would be writing an American story, he replied, "You see, I write the story and then fill in the place, like blanks in a railway form.

The places don't count so much. The story is the thing." He was then asked,

> But you will give your people some of their own types, with characteristic dialect, will you not?   And won't that require you to select your scenes first?

He replied:

> No, not entirely.   Even that can be filled in.   It is astonishing how much can be filled in.   I rewrote one of my books three times, and each time it was a different book.   I had filled in, and filled in, until the original book wasn't there.   It had evaporated through the blanks, and I had an entirely new book.   I shall write my story, and then lay the scene where I want it, and, if necessary, change other things to suit the places.[268]

It appears that he really did think that he could create with an almost complete independence of places and circumstances. It is hardly surprising that his "original book" (it has been shown that he had lately been working on *The Mysterious Stranger)* had "evaporated through the blanks." What is surprising is that he should have been so confident of his ability to create good literature in a void, apart from any essential background. How could he have so strangely mistaken the weakness of his art for its strength?

Albert Paine, who had every opportunity to know the later Mark Twain, wrote that he "lived curiously apart from the actualities of life. Dwelling mainly among his philosophies and speculations, he observed vaguely, or minutely, what went on about him; but in either case the fact took a place, not in the actual world, but in a world within."[269] Paine also made this perceptive comment:

> Insubstantial and deceptive as was this inner world of his, to him it must have been much more real than the world of flitting physical shapes about him. . . . [Y]ou realized, at last, that he was placing you and seeing you not as a part of the material landscape, but as an item of his own inner world.[270]

Given such a freedom from the "world of flitting physical shapes," perhaps Mark Twain's art could not have failed to arrive at something like the solipsism that it reaches in the "dream ending." There it is disclosed that the only world is the story-teller's "world within." And what role is possible for an artist who has no use for the outer reality, "the material landscape"? He may be "but a *thought*—a vagrant thought, a useless thought, a homeless thought, wandering forlorn among the empty eternities!"[271]

The same vacuity provides the base, or rather the *baselessness,* of events in the "Print Shop" chapter that Mark Twain wrote at Stormfield as his latest work on the story. The famous dead of many centuries flit by as dim and shadowy apparitions; there is little description, and there is no scenery at all in the "empty & soundless world" that remains as a vacant realm after a fade-away from the last lingering traces of reality.

Yet such an interpretation—that Twain's art lost contact with reality—must not be pushed too far. It has been noted that he could speak of a solipsistic view of life as someone's "foible." And he was probably more at home in the real world than his own words would sometimes suggest. Certainly he recognized the existence of other persons in the world. And it is greatly to his credit that he desired for them the same freedom that he claimed for himself. Dorothy Quick, who as a little girl enjoyed Mark Twain's friendship, has related that once in 1908 when he took her to a circus, Mark Twain became somewhat melancholy after seeing an elephant perform upon cues from its trainer. He remarked that he always felt "sad to see anything brought down from its high estate—or something meant to be great that doesn't know its own power."[272] The elephant, he said, could probably have stampeded all the people who were present; however, it did not know its possibilities and so did tricks at the crack of a whip. And he was further saddened to think how many men were, like the elephant, unaware of their great powers. They toiled at low tasks, as they were ordered, although they had within them, all along, "the driving power of the universe."[273] But he told Dorothy that she needn't worry; that he knew *his* powers—and he would see to it that she knew hers. He was thus proposing to play, in actual life, the role of the mysterious stranger, revealing to a young person the limitless power of the creative mind. One of the things he told her was "No matter what happens, you must write,"[274] an injunction that eventually led to the writing of her book about Mark Twain.

Mark Twain was the mysterious stranger. And he played his role wonderfully to the last.

NOTES

1 See Bernard DeVoto, *Mark Twain at Work* (Cambridge, Mass.: Harvard University Press, 1942), pp. vii-ix.

2 For an excellent summary of the prevailing critical view, see Dixon Wecter, "Mark Twain," *Literary History of the United States,* Revised ed. (New York: Macmillan, 1953), pp. 937-939. Wecter calls *The Mysterious Stranger* the "greatest story of Mark Twain's later period" and follows DeVoto in stating that it "wins at last the personal answer for which he sought so desperately." See also, for recent and very capable discussions of this story, Kenneth S. Lynn, *Mark Twain and Southwestern Humor* (Boston: Little, Brown, and Co., 1959), pp. 270-285; Pascal Covici, Jr., *Mark Twain's Humor: The Image of a World* (Dallas: Southern Methodist University Press, 1962), pp. 227-236; and Albert E. Stone, Jr., *The Innocent Eye: Childhood in Mark Twain's Imagination* (New Haven: Yale University Press, 1961), pp. 228-263.

3 "Hannibal" is paginated 1-136 but has 139 actual pages: there are two page-sequences numbered 95-97, the one immediately following the other. "Eseldorf," paginated 1-423, has 423 actual pages: there is an inserted page 58½, an instance of duplicate pagination (two pages numbered 140), and a skipping of 373 and 374 in the numbering. "Print Shop," consisting of pp. 23-587 and two separately paginated fragments of six and eight pages respectively, has many discontinuities: there are many inserted pages as well as relatively large gaps in pagination, the actual number of pages being 534. The 22-page initial chapter of "Eseldorf" was "borrowed" by Twain for use as the first chapter of "Print Shop"; thus, the latter manuscript begins at p. 23.

4 *The Mysterious Stranger* was first published serially in *Harper's Magazine,* beginning with the May, 1916, issue.

5 *Definitive Edition,* XXVII, pp. 3-4. This edition, used for this and subsequent references to the published works unless otherwise noted, is *The Writings of Mark Twain* (New York: Gabriel Wells, 1922-1925), 37 vols., hereinafter cited as *Writings.*

6 *Writings,* XXVII, p. 77.

7 *Ibid.,* p. 87.

8 *Ibid.,* p. 80.

9 *Ibid.,* pp. 13-21.

10 *Ibid.,* p. 80.

11 *Ibid.,* p. 51.

12 *Ibid.,* p. 26.

13 *Ibid.,* pp. 83-87.

14 *Ibid.,* pp. 121-131.

15 *Ibid.,* pp. 137-140.

16 Bernard DeVoto, *Mark Twain at Work* (Cambridge, Mass.; Harvard University Press, 1942), pp. 105-115. Twain finished the writing of *Following the Equator* on May 18, 1897; see *Mark Twain's Notebook,* ed. Albert Bigelow Paine (New York: Harper & Brothers, 1935), p. 327.

17 *Mark Twain at Work,* p. 112. See also Bernard DeVoto, *Mark Twain in Eruption* (New York: Grosset & Dunlap, 1940), p. 198*n.*

18 *Mark Twain at Work,* pp. 127-128.

19 *Ibid.,* p. 117.

20 *Ibid.,* p. 117.

21 *Ibid.,* p. 127.

22 *Ibid.,* p. 130.

23 *Ibid.,* p. ix.

24 *Ibid.,* p. 127.

25 *Mark Twain: A Biography* (New York: Gabriel Wells, 1923), 4 vols., III, p. 1067.

26 *Writings,* XXVII, p. ix.

27 *Ibid.,* p. ix.

28 *Ibid.,* pp. ix-x.

29 *Mark Twain's Notebook,* p. 369.

30 See *Mark Twain at Work,* p. 105. DeVoto under-rated Paine as a biographer and as a critic.

31 *Ibid.,* p. 130.

32 DeVoto considered—correctly, it appears—that it was during or following the year 1896 (in that year Twain's daughter Susy died) that Mark Twain began to make much use of pessimistic themes and "symbols of despair" which were to find expression in the variants of *The Mysterious Stranger,* as well as in other related manuscripts (see *Mark Twain at Work,* p. 109). An examination of the manuscripts in this "Despair Group," as it might be termed, disclosed no evidence that any of them had been written earlier than 1896. It is, however, true that many of his earlier writings contain scattered passages that are in the vein of his later pessimism. "The despair expressed in Mark Twain's late work had its origins in an intellectual crisis antedating the period of his personal

misfortunes," as Henry Nash Smith has recently observed in *Mark Twain: The Development of a Writer* (Cambridge, Mass.: Harvard University Press, 1962), p. 186.

33 *Mark Twain at Work*, p. 115.

34 *Writings*, XXVII, p. 3.

35 See *Mark Twain's Notebook*, p. 339.

36 Max Lederer, "Mark Twain in Vienna," *Mark Twain Quarterly*, VII (Summer-Fall, 1945), p. 2. This useful article is mainly a digest of news items about Mark Twain as reported in the *Neue Freie Presse*.

37 *Ibid.*, p. 2.

38 *Ibid.*, p. 2.

39 *Ibid.*, p. 3.

40 *Mark Twain: A Biography*, III, pp. 1050-1052.

41 These memoranda are not in *Mark Twain's Notebook* but are available in the holographic notebooks and in full typescript copies in the Mark Twain Papers at the University of California, Berkeley. See Typescript 32b (II), pp. 44-48.

42 "Mark Twain in Vienna," pp. 3-4.

43 In *Literary Essays, Writings*, XXII, pp. 197-243.

44 *Ibid.;* the name "Wohlmeyer" appears on p. 227 and p. 229, "Fuchs" appears on p. 240, and "Lueger" is mentioned fifteen times in pp. 224-233. The passage of "Eseldorf" in which a character named Fuchs is presented will be further discussed in the next chapter.

45 Beginning on p. 17 of the 22-page chapter, "Adolf" appears in the holograph as originally written. "Lueger" was written initially on pp. 5, 7, 8, and 10 and then crossed out with wavy lines and replaced with "Adolf."

46 Fourteenth ed., II, p. 77.

47 *Writings*, XXII, pp. 263-287. On the first page of this article, he indicates that it was written in response to inquiries he had received concerning what he had said about the Jews in "Stirring Times in Austria."

48 See *Mark Twain: A Biography*, III, pp. 1145-1148.

49 *Britannica*, s. v. "Lueger, Karl," describes him as "zealous" in his religious duties, wishing to "capture the university" for his church.

50 Typescript 32b (II), p. 46. This note bears comparison with "Eseldorf," p. 6, where Father Lueger is said to have "belonged to the village Council, & lorded it there, & played smart dodges that carried his projects through." Copyright 1963, Mark Twain Co.

51 *Writings*, XXII, p. 229.

52 *Ibid.*, p. 231.

53 *Ibid.*, p. 227.

54 *Britannica*, II, p. 77.

55 *Writings*, XXVII, p. 7.

[56] *Mark Twain's Notebook,* p. 340.

[57] "Eseldorf," p. 5.   Copyright 1963, Mark Twain Co.

[58] *Writings,* XXVII, p. 30.

[59] "Eseldorf," p. 65.   Copyright 1963, Mark Twain Co.

[60] Notes for *The Mysterious Stranger,* numbered DV 327bb in the Mark Twain Papers.   Copyright 1963, Mark Twain Co.

[61] *Mark Twain's Letters,* ed.   Albert Bigelow Paine   (New York: Gabriel Wells, 1923), II, p. 647.

[62] See "Stirring Times in Austria," pp. 236-243.

[63] *Writings,* XXVII, p. 3.

[64] *Writings,* XXVII, p. 8.

[65] *Ibid.,* p. 34.

[66] In his notes, Twain listed the new name for the good priest as "Father Kitchelt."   This name does not appear in "Eseldorf," and it seems that before beginning that version he had decided to call him "Father Peter."

The "pre-Eseldorf" pages were originally numbered 12, 16-18, 20, 20-32 (two pages were numbered 20), and 34; in revision, these numbers in "Eseldorf" became, respectively, 53, 56-72, and 74.

[67] As incorporated in "Eseldorf" and in *The Mysterious Stranger,* with revisions, this material may be found in *Writings,* XXVII, p. 24 and pp. 27-34.

[68] "Hellfire Hotchkiss," an incomplete, unpublished story, was written at Weggis; see *Mark Twain: A Biography,* III, p. 1045.   Other manuscripts which may have been written there and which were searched for evidence of possible use of the buff paper of "Eseldorf" include "The Enchanted Sea Wilderness," "Villagers of 1840-43," "An Adventure in Remote Seas," "Statement of the Edwardses," "Which Was the Dream?" "Indiantown," and "Tom Sawyer's Conspiracy."   All of these manuscripts are in the Mark Twain Papers.   Most of them include pages that are on a cross-barred paper which Twain used extensively at Weggis and perhaps there only.   But no paper matching that of pp. 1-85 and 377-386 of "Eseldorf" was found.

He took residence at Weggis on July 18, 1897; see *Mark Twain's Notebook,* p. 331.

[69] *Mark Twain, Business Man* (Boston: Little, Brown, and Co., 1946), p. 14.

[70] *Ibid.,* p. 13.

[71] *Ibid.,* pp. 45-46.

[72] Other possible sources are discussed by Coleman O. Parsons, "The Background of *"The Mysterious Stranger,"* *American Literature,* XXXII (March, 1960), pp. 55-74.   See also Carroll D. Laverty, "The Genesis of

The Mysterious Stranger," *Mark Twain Quarterly*, VIII (Spring-Summer, 1947), pp. 15-19.

73 *Mark Twain's Notebook*, p. 256.

74 Typescript 31 (II), p. 36.

75 Edmund Gurney, F. W. H. Myers, and Frank Podmore, *Phantasms of the Living* (London: Trubner, 1886).

76 *Writings*, XXII, p. 135.

77 *Mark Twain's Notebook*, pp. 349-350.

78 *Writings*, XXVII, pp. 9-10.

79 *The Principles of Psychology*, Authorized Edition (New York: Henry Holt & Co., 1890), II, p. 294.

80 *Mark Twain's Notebook*, p. 352.

81 *Ibid.*, p. 352.

82 *Writings*, XXVII, p. 27.   The resemblance of this description to that of the dream self in the entry of January 7 is noted by Covici, *Mark Twain's Humor*, p. 239.   Covici considers that Satan is a "projection of Theodor's destructive conscience."

83 *Mark Twain's Notebook*, p. 312.

84 *Mark Twain's Letters*, II, p. 641.

85 *Mark Twain-Howells Letters*, ed. Henry Nash Smith and William M. Gibson with the assistance of Frederick Anderson (Cambridge, Mass.: Harvard University Press, 1960), II, pp. 664-665.

86 *Ibid.*, p. 665.

87 Mark Twain, *Letters From the Earth*, ed. Bernard DeVoto (New York: Harper & Row, 1962), p. 229.   The preface by Henry Nash Smith explains that DeVoto edited this volume in 1939 but did not then publish it because of Clara Clemens' objections, which she later withdrew.

88 *Writings*, XXVII, p. 20.

89 *Ibid.*, p. 26.

90 *Letters From the Earth*, pp. 225-226.

91 *Ibid.*, p. 228.

92 *Writings*, XXVII, pp. 50-51.

93 *Letters From the Earth*, p. 222n.   DeVoto stated here that the clippings "probably referred to the Cretan revolt of 1897."   However, in his notes at the end of the volume, he said that this piece probably belonged "to the period 1905-1909," although it might "go back to 1897" (p. 292).   Inasmuch as he believed "Eseldorf" to have been written as the last of the versions, he apparently found it difficult to accept an early dating of material so closely related to "Eseldorf."

94 Ibid., p. 227.

95 Typescript 32a (II), p. 37.   Lynn, *Mark Twain and Southwestern Humor*, p. 280, cites this note but supposes that it was not followed up with further plotting of such a story until nearly "a year and a half later."

[96] See "Letters to Satan," *Writings,* XXIX, pp. 211-220.

[97] See *Mark Twain's Notebook,* p. 331.

[98] *Writings,* XXIX, p. 212.

[99] *Writings,* XXVII, p. 114.

[100] See Typescript 32b (I), p. 24.   Twain noted that he had begun the story on August 4.

[101] "Hellfire Hotchkiss," pp. 33-34.

[102] *Writings,* XXVII, pp. 85-86.

[103] "Villagers of 1840-1843," p. 23.

[104] *Ibid.,* p. 10.

[105] *Writings,* XXVII, p. 85.

[106] See *Mark Twain: A Biography,* III, pp. 1038-1042, and Paul Fatout, *Mark Twain on the Lecture Circuit* (Bloomington: Indiana University Press, 1960), pp. 241-271.

[107] *Texas Studies in English,* XXXVII (1958), pp. 3-23.

[108] A copy of this letter is in the Mark Twain Papers.

[109] *Mark Twain's Letters,* II, pp. 641-642.

[110] See Caroline Thomas Harnsberger, *Mark Twain: Family Man* (New York: Citadel Press, 1960), p. 168.   When Clara Clemens brought her mother the news of Susy's death, "Mrs. Clemens paled until it seemed she must faint, then cried out: 'I don't believe it!' She and Clara *never* believed it."

[111] *Mark Twain's Notebook,* p. 337.

[112] Notes for *The Mysterious Stranger,* DV 327 bb.

[113] The holograph is in the Mark Twain Papers.   See also *Mark Twain: A Biography,* IV, pp. 1238-1239; 1663-1670.

[114] The holograph is in the Mark Twain Papers.   DeVoto briefly discusses this story in *Mark Twain at Work,* p. 119.

[115] *Writings,* XXVII, p. 76.

[116] Notes for *The Mysterious Stranger,* DV 327 bb.

[117] "Mark Twain in Vienna," p. 2.

[118] *Writings,* XXIX, p. xxxv.

[119] *Writings,* XXIII, p. x.

[120] *Ibid.,* p. x.

[121] *Writings,* XXII, p. 230.

[122] *Ibid.,* p. 199.

[123] *Writings,* XXIII, p. 37.

[124] *Ibid.,* p. xi.

[125] In *The Mysterious Stranger,* Theodor, the naive boy-narrator, does not snicker; however, the reader, who also "looks on," is in effect invited to do so.

[126] These manuscripts in the Mark Twain Papers are "Lecture Times," DV 274 (6), and "Ralph Keeler," DV 274 (7), used in *Mark Twain's*

Autobiography (New York: Gabriel Wells, 1924), I, pp. 147-153 and 154-164. Paine, who edited the *Autobiography,* tried to present the materials "in the order in which they were written" (Vol. I, 1*n*); he placed these two selections consecutively just preceding an item—"Beauties of the German Language"—which bears Twain's internal dating of February 3, 1898. Moreover, Twain wrote in his notebook, some time between December 1 and 11, 1897, "Ralph Keeler, Gloverson and His Silent Partner; librarian had a copy" (Typescript 32b (II), p. 50), recalling incidents that figure in "Ralph Keeler." He would in all probability have written of these matters soon after thus gathering his recollections of them. It appears that he had and was using, near the end of 1897, the "rare" buff paper of "Eseldorf." Copyright 1963, Mark Twain Co.

126a More precisely, a change of inks on the last page of this sequence (p. 386, originally 93) indicates that he broke off in the middle of this page, then filled out the rest of it upon taking up the story later. Mark Twain had been leading up to the disclosure of Father Peter's "happy insanity"; it is with this disclosure that the later written part begins.

127 The paper of pp. 86-376 and 387-392 is of a light-weight, cream-colored stock, 5″ by 8″, with vertical watermark lines spaced 1″ apart; that of pp. 393-423 is of stock of the same weight, ochre, 5″ by 7⅞″, with vertical watermark lines spaced $1\frac{5}{16}$″ apart. The ink on both papers is gray.

128 The writing of pp. 1-85 brought the story to a point about one-third of the way through Chapter V (*Writings,* XXVII, pp. 3-40); pp. 377-386 (originally pp. 84-93) became part of Chapter X (*Ibid.,* pp. 124-128).

129 Typescript 32b (II), p. 53. Copyright 1963, Mark Twain Co.

130 *Mark Twain-Howells Letters,* II, p. 670.

131 Paine, *Mark Twain: A Biography,* III, p. 1067, observes: "A good deal of work done at this period did not find its way into print," and, in his further discussion of Twain's work at the beginning of 1898, refers to his "interest in Satan" and mentions the "three bulky manuscripts in which he has attempted to set down some episodes in the life of one 'Young Satan.' "

132 An indication of his probable output per day may be found in his observation, made in April, 1904, that he was then averaging "fourteen hundred words per sitting of four or five hours" (*Mark Twain's Autobiography,* I, p. 246). In early January, 1898, he would by working "long hours" have been producing considerably more. Even after allowance for his tendency to overestimate his output—see Walter Blair, "When Was *Huckleberry Finn* Written?" *American Literature,* XXX (March, 1958), p. 5—it appears that he could have written 12,350 words in less than two weeks. The estimated wordage of these 95 pp. has been computed using an average of 130 words per page, based upon a word count. These

figures are higher than those that Blair found to be representative of Twain's practice at an earlier time (*Ibid.*); however, the handwriting became decidedly smaller in the later years.

133 "Eseldorf," pp. 14-16. Copyright 1963, Mark Twain Co.

134 *Writings*, XXII, p. 243.

135 *Mark Twain's Notebook*, p. 343.

136 *Writings*, XXII, p. 265.

137 *Mark Twain's Notebook*, p. 369.

138 Notes for *The Mysterious Stranger*, DV 327c.

139 "Hannibal," pp. 1-136.

140 Notes for *The Mysterious Stranger*, DV 327c.

141 *Writings*, XXVII, p. 17.

142 The initial working notes for "Eseldorf" seem to reveal that Twain had in that version identified himself quite closely with the boy-narrator; as has been shown above, he wrote "Theodor Fischer [Tom] Huck (I)." Copyright 1963, Mark Twain Co.

143 *Mark Twain-Howells Letters*, II, pp. 698-699.

144 Notes for *The Mysterious Stranger*, DV 327bb. Copyright 1963, Mark Twain Co.

145 See *Writings*, XXVII, pp. 40-44.

146 "Eseldorf," pp. 110-139.

147 *Ibid.*, pp. 167-229.

148 Notes for *The Mysterious Stranger*, DV 327bb. Copyright 1963, Mark Twain Co.

149 *Writings*, XXVII, p. 76.

150 *Mark Twain-Howells Letters*, II, p. 710.

151 *Writings*, XXVII, p. 34. The reference to Marie Lueger appears on p. 73 of the manuscript. This page was not a part of the "pre-Eseldorf" draft and was not repaginated as were the sheets borrowed from that draft.

152 *Ibid.*, p. 34. This passage is on p. 74 of the manuscript and was originally numbered 34 in the "pre-Eseldorf" draft.

153 In *Mark Twain, Business Man*, pp. 15-16.

154 *Ibid.*, p. 14.

155 Notes for *The Mysterious Stranger*, DV 327bb. Copyright 1963, Mark Twain Co.

156 "Eseldorf," p. 229 *verso; Writings*, XXVII, p. 76.

157 See Philip S. Foner, *Mark Twain: Social Critic* (New York: International, 1958), p. 253, but also *Britannica*, V, p. 532.

158 This 9,200-word sequence includes Satan's exposition of deterministic doctrines, the episode of Nikolaus's and Lisa's drownings, and Frau Brandt's blaspheming and her subsequent execution by fire at the stake. ("Eseldorf," pp. 229-291; *Writings*, XXVII, pp. 76-107).

159 To bring such materials into a tale of events in Austria in 1590 (see *Writings*, XXVII, p. 3) required, of course, some contriving. See n. 162 below.

160 *Writings*, XXVII, p. 111.

161 "Eseldorf," p. 301. Copyright 1963, Mark Twain Co.

162 *Ibid.*, p. 364. Copyright 1963, Mark Twain Co. In writing "Eseldorf," Twain first indicated May, 1702, as the time of the action; thereafter, he deleted that date and changed the time to the winter of 1490. Then, in the typescript copy, he struck out "1490" and inserted "1590." As a result of these changes, the published story now begins, "It was in 1590—winter" (*Writings*, XXVII, p. 3), though the action, as Twain had planned and written "Eseldorf," began "one May night" (*Ibid.*, p. 10) in 1702. In predicting events of 1900, Satan was thus looking forward approximately two centuries.

163 *Mark Twain's Letters*, II, p. 699.

164 For an excellent study of Twain's views and writings concerning imperialism, see William M. Gibson, "Mark Twain and Howells: Anti-Imperialists," *New England Quarterly*, XX (December, 1947), pp. 435-470. With reference to Twain's letter of August 12 to Twichell, quoted above, Gibson comments that "on the day before international troops relieved the legations in Peking, not many weeks before he sailed for the United States, Mark Twain clearly aligned himself with "the person sitting in darkness" (p. 444).

165 *Mark Twain: Life as I Find It*, ed. Charles Neider (Garden City: Hanover House, 1961), p. 325. Neider has reprinted selected press interviews of Twain.

166 This letter is quoted in part in *Mark Twain: A Biography*, III, p. 1109; Paine says it was written "in midsummer." Twain reported that his wife Olivia was "enchanted with the place," which had large, attractive grounds. He was writing regularly and was "the only person . . . ever in the house in the daytime."

167 A copy of this letter is in the Mark Twain Papers.

168 "Eseldorf," p. 399. Copyright 1963, Mark Twain Co.

169 *Writings*, XXVII, p. 131.

170 This unposted letter of 14 pp., actually an essay titled "The Missionary in World-Politics," is addressed to Moberly Bell and dated "Dollis Hill House, Kilburn N. W. Monday [summer-fall, 1900]." The holograph is in the Mark Twain Papers.

171 This manuscript (DV 239, Mark Twain Papers) may be dated by Twain's statement that he is to "begin a sea-voyage seventeen days hence" (p. 14); he sailed on October 6 (see *Mark Twain: A Biography*, III, p. 1110) and would have been writing on or about September 19, 1900.

172 New York *World,* October 14, 1900; reprinted in *Mark Twain: Life as I Find It,* p. 331.

173 New York *Herald,* October 16, 1900; reprinted in *Mark Twain: Life as I Find It,* pp. 335-336.

174 *Ibid.,* p. 336.

175 For a discussion of these notebook entries and of the evidence regarding the "Fifty Years Later" story that Mark Twain may have written, see *Mark Twain-Howells Letters,* II, n. 1, p. 748.

176 See *Writings,* XXVII, p. 21.

177 Typescript of "Eseldorf" (DV 327a, Mark Twain Papers), p. 24. Copyright 1963, Mark Twain Co.

178 *Ibid.,* p. 25. Copyright 1963, Mark Twain Co.

179 See Walter Blair, *Mark Twain & Huck Finn* (Berkeley: University of California Press, 1960), p. 253.

180 See *Mark Twain at Work,* p. 62, and *Mark Twain & Huck Finn,* pp. 249-259.

181 *Mark Twain in Eruption,* p. 199.

182 *Mark Twain: A Biography,* III, p. 1181.

183 New York *World,* September 7, 1902; reprinted in *Mark Twain: Life as I Find It,* p. 361.

184 William Dean Howells, *My Mark Twain: Reminiscences and Criticisms* (New York: Harper & Brothers, 1910), p. 90. See also *Mark Twain: A Biography,* III, p. 1177.

185 This six-page fragment is presently placed with "Eseldorf" (DV 327, Mark Twain Papers).

186 See *Mark Twain-Howells Letters,* II, p. 772.

187 Mark Twain may have taken "Stein," the name of the kindly master, from "Liechtenstein," the name of the Austrian prince who probably inspired the characterization of good Father Peter; the prince opposed Dr. Karl Lueger in Austrian politics very much as, in "Eseldorf," Father Peter opposed Father Lueger (Adolf) in religious matters. See the discussion of these matters in Chapter 2 above.

188 "Print Shop" (DV 328, Mark Twain Papers), p. 24.

189 "Eseldorf," p. 2. Copyright 1963, Mark Twain Co.

190 DV 328a, Mark Twain Papers.

191 *Mark Twain: A Biography,* I, pp. 76-77.

192 These notes are presently stored with the "Print Shop" holograph.

193 A systematic search of the correspondence in the Mark Twain Papers revealed the first indication of her having assumed her secretaryship to be a letter that she wrote, concerning some busines transactions, to F. G. Whitmore on November 12, 1902. From that time on, her presence is shown by other letters and notes in her large, distinctive handwriting.

Internal evidence also shows that the greater part of "Print Shop" could not have been written until 1902 or thereafter. Beginning on p. 145 of this manuscript, he introduced clippings from a religious pamphlet that had been issued by the Benedictine Sisters of Perpetual Adoration of Clyde, Missouri. The pamphlet explains that their chapel had been extensively damaged by repeated strokes of lighting. Twain represented the clipped passages as a speech by Father Peter (who had been brought into "Print Shop" in the borrowed first chapter of "Eseldorf") maintaining that these destructive bolts were actually providential and miraculous and expressed the Lord's will that the Sisters should have a new chapel. The rest of the pamphlet has also survived, and it contains a testimonial letter dated February 10, 1902; it is thus certain that Twain wrote this and the following part of "Print Shop" after that date.

194 See *Mark Twain: A Biography*, III, pp. 1238-1239; IV, pp. 1663-1670.

195 A typescript copy of this letter is in the Mark Twain Papers. Copyright 1963, Mark Twain Co.

196 See *Mark Twain: A Biography*, III, pp. 1205-1211.

197 *Mark Twain's Letters*, II, p. 749.

198 *Mark Twain-Howells Letters*, II, p. 779.

199 This unpublished manuscript, known as the "George Harrison" story, contains more than 100,000 words.

200 See *Mark Twain: A Biography*, III, p. 1212. The usage of "Katzenyammer" may be found in *Writings*, XXIV, p. 40.

201 *Mark Twain: A Biography*, III, pp. 1194-1196.

202 *Ibid.*, pp. 1205-1208.

203 There are, in the part of "Print Shop" preceding p. 433, some inserted pages that are of the white paper and the black ink that Twain used in the 1905-written part (pp. 433-587). He evidently went back to make revisions.

204 This manuscript, designated as Paine No. 44 in the Mark Twain Papers, has been published in *Writings*, XXIV, pp. 229-242.

205 To Dr. Laing Gordon, in the Mark Twain Papers, unpublished.

206 DV 373, Mark Twain Papers.

207 Notebook 37 (1904). Some of the entries made between the above-mentioned dates have been published in *Mark Twain's Notebook*, pp. 386-387.

208 The different colors may best be compared by looking at pages on which these inks have been smeared. See, for such samples, the following: p. 132 (dark blue); p. 172 (vivid light blue); p. 215 (purplish blue); p. 5 of the separately paginated 6-page fragment (purplish blue).

209 See *Writings*, XXVII, p. 138.

210 Paine No. 42, Mark Twain Papers; *Writings*, XXV, pp. 262-264.

211 *Writings,* XXVII, pp. 136-137.

212 Copyright 1963, Mark Twain Co.

213 *Mark Twain's Letters,* II, pp. 755-756.

214 A typescript copy of this letter is in the Mark Twain Papers; the original is in the Yale Collection. Copyright 1963, Mark Twain Co.

215 *Writings,* XXVII, p. 138.

216 *Ibid.,* p. 137.

217 *Mark Twain's Notebook,* p. 320.

218 Typescript 31 (II), p. 50.

219 Notes for *The Mysterious Stranger,* DV 327c.

220 *Writings,* XXVII, p. 140.

221 See *Mark Twain: A Biography,* III, pp. 1067-1068.

222 Authorized Edition (Boston: published by the author, 1875), p. 250.

223 *Ibid.,* p. 280.

224 See *Mark Twain's Letters,* II, p. 783; *Mark Twain: A Biography,* III, pp. 1238-1239.

225 *Mark Twain's Notebook,* p. 170.

226 *Writings,* XX, p. 114.

227 *Mark Twain: A Biography,* p. 1663. Paine published here an excerpt from "3,000 Years Among the Microbes."

228 *Ibid.,* p. 1666.

229 A typescript copy of this letter is in the Mark Twain Papers.

230 DV 347, Mark Twain Papers.

231 A typescript copy of this letter is in the Mark Twain Papers.

232 Copyright 1963, Mark Twain Co.

233 Copyright 1963, Mark Twain Co.

234 Except for a few preliminary pages, all of "3,000 Years Among the Microbes" is written with this placement. So are other manuscripts written that summer, including "The War Prayer" (Paine No. 135; *Writings,* XXIX, pp. 394-398).

235 Copyright 1963, Mark Twain Co.

236 *Mark Twain's Letters,* II, p. 77.

237 A copy of this letter is in the Mark Twain Papers.

238 Typescript copy, Mark Twain Papers, p. 1367. Copyright 1963, Mark Twain Co.

239 Mark Twain to J. Y. M. MacAlister. A photostatic copy of this letter is in the Mark Twain Papers.

240 A copy of this letter is in the Mark Twain Papers.

241 V, 1, 50-57.

242 *Mark Twain's Letters,* II, pp. 783-784.

243 *Ibid.,* II, p. 795.

244 *Ibid.*

245 *Mark Twain in Eruption,* pp. 198-199.

246 A copy of this letter is the Mark Twain Papers; the original is in the Harvard College Library.

247 Published in the *North American Review* (August 2, 1907), p. 689.

248 A photostatic copy of this letter is in the Mark Twain Papers.

249 *Mark Twain's Notebook,* pp. 369-370.

250 "Print Shop," 8-page fragment, p. 8. Copyright 1963, Mark Twain Co.

251 III, p. 1034. Some idea of the extent to which Twain's handwriting changed in the latter years, and of the possibility of dating manuscripts in terms of such changes, may be gained by comparing the specimen of 1908 with that of October 25, 1897 (approximately the time of his earliest work upon *The Mysterious Stranger*), as presented in *Mark Twain's Letters,* II, p. 648.

252 Paine No. 237, Mark Twain Papers.

253 The holograph of this letter is in the Mark Twain Papers. It is headed, "P. S. to my secretary's letter," and was apparently written to accompany a letter by Isabel Lyon, who had been handling other correspondence of Mark Twain relating to the Children's Educational Theatre of New York. It has been published with some omissions in *Mark Twain's Letters,* II, pp. 818-821.

254 He may have first gotten the idea of the dream-pageant by witnessing Wilbrandt's play "The Master of Palmyra"; he wrote that it had given him "the sense of the passage of a dimly connected procession of dream-pictures" ("About Play-acting," *Writings,* XXIII, p. 214). See also *Mark Twain-Howells Letters,* II, Letter No. 533, n. 7, p. 686, and Coleman O. Parsons, "The Background of *The Mysterious Stranger,*" p. 59. The quotations from "Print Shop" are copyright 1963, Mark Twain Co.

255 *Writings,* XXVII, p. 140.

256 "Print Shop," p. 513. Copyright 1963, Mark Twain Co.

257 *Ibid.,* p. 519. Copyright 1963, Mark Twain Co.

258 *Ibid.,* p. 526. Copyright 1963, Mark Twain Co.

259 *Writings,* XXVII, p. 138.

260 The chapter written in 1908 was not designated as a conclusion but was headed merely "Chap." He commonly indicated chapter beginnings in this way, adding numbers later. Also at the top of p. 1 of this fragment he wrote "Mysterious Stranger" and, immediately below, "added." Copyright 1963, Mark Twain Co.

261 This identification is discussed in Chapter 5. See also n. 260.

262 *Mark Twain at Work,* p. 127.

263 *Ibid.,* pp. 114-115.

264 "The Structural Problem of *The Mysterious Stranger,*" *Studies in Philology,* XLIX (January, 1952), p. 102.

265 Consciously or unconsciously, he may have projected his own situation in the last fully developed incident of the "Eseldorf" version, that of the magic tree that Satan caused to grow in India and to bear a seemingly inexhaustible supply of "fruits of many kinds and colors." After a foreigner had claimed possession of the tree and had struck Satan, the "fruits rotted on the branches, and the leaves withered and fell." Satan then admonished "the foreigner": "Take good care of the tree, for its health and yours are bound together. It will never bear again, but if you tend it well it will live long. Water its roots once in each hour every night. . . . If you fail only once in any night, the tree will die, and you likewise" (*Writings,* XXVII, p. 134).

266 *Writings,* XXVII, p. 80.

267 Pascal Covici, Jr., *Mark Twain's Humor: The Image of a World,* p. 247.

268 *Mark Twain: Life as I Find It,* pp. 335-336.

269 *Mark Twain: A Biography,* IV, p. 1519.

270 *Ibid.,* p. 1520.

271 *Writings,* XXVII, p. 140.

272 Dorothy Quick, *Enchantment: A Little Girl's Friendship With Mark Twain* (Norman: University of Oklahoma Press, 1961), p. 160.

273 *Ibid.,* p. 160.

274 *Ibid.,* p. 218.

A SELECTED BIBLIOGRAPHY

Unpublished Material

Albert B. Paine Collection, Huntington Library, San Marino, California.

Henry W. and Albert A. Berg Collection, New York Public Library, New York, N. Y.

Mark Twain Papers, General Library, University of California, Berkeley.

Books and Articles

Altick, Richard D. "Mark Twain's Despair: An Explanation in Terms of His Humanity." *South Atlantic Quarterly*, XXXIV (October, 1935), 359-367.

Andrews, Kenneth R. *Nook Farm: Mark Twain's Hartford Circle*. Cambridge, Mass.: Harvard University Press, 1950.

Bellamy, Gladys Carmen. *Mark Twain as a Literary Artist*. Norman: University of Oklahoma Press, 1950.

Blair, Walter. *Mark Twain and Huck Finn*. Berkeley: University of California Press, 1960.

————. "When Was *Huckleberry Finn* Written?" *American Literature*, XXX (March, 1958), 1-25.

Brashear, Minnie M. *Mark Twain, Son of Missouri*. Chapel Hill: University of North Carolina Press, 1934.

Brooks, Van Wyck. *The Ordeal of Mark Twain*. Revised edition. New York: E. P. Dutton, 1933.

Burhans, Clinton S. "The Sober Affirmation of Mark Twain's Hadleyburg." *American Literature*, XXXIV (November, 1962), 375-385.

Canby, Henry Seidel. *Turn West, Turn East*. Boston: Houghton Mifflin, 1951.

Carter, Paul J., Jr. "Olivia Clemens Edits *Following the Equator*." *American Literature*, XXX (May, 1958), 194-209.

"China." *Encyclopædia Britannica*. Chicago: Britannica, Inc., 1950. Volume V.

Clemens, Clara. *Awake to a Perfect Day*. New York: Citadel Press, 1956.

Covici, Pascal, Jr. *Mark Twain's Humor: The Image of a World*. Dallas: Southern Methodist University Press, 1962.

Cowper, Frederick A. G. "The Hermit Story, as Used by Voltaire and Mark Twain," in *Papers . . . in Honor of . . . Charles Frederick Johnson,* ed. Odell Shepard and Arthur Adams. Hartford, Conn., 1928, pp. 313-337.

DeVoto, Bernard, *Mark Twain at Work*. Cambridge, Mass.: Harvard University Press, 1942.

————. *Mark Twain's America*. Boston: Little, Brown, 1935.

Eddy, Mary Baker. *Science and Health with Key to the Scriptures*. Authorized edition. Boston: published by the author, 1875.

Fatout, Paul. *Mark Twain on the Lecture Circuit*. Bloomington: Indiana University Press, 1960.

Ferguson, DeLancey. *Mark Twain: Man and Legend*. Indianapolis: Bobbs Merrill, 1943.

Foner, Philip S. *Mark Twain: Social Critic*. New York: International, 1958.

Friedrich, Gerhard. "Erosion of Values in Twain's Humor." *The CEA Critic,* XXII (September, 1960), 1-8.

Fussell, E. S. "The Structural Problem of *The Mysterious Stranger*." *Studies in Philology,* XLIX (January, 1952), 95-104.

Gerber, John C. "Mark Twain's Use of the Comic Pose." *Publications of the Modern Language Association of America,* LXXVII (June, 1962), 297-304.

Gibson, William M. "Mark Twain and Howells: Anti-Imperialists," *New England Quarterly,* XX (December, 1947), 435-470.

Goold, Edgar H., Jr. "Mark Twain on the Writing of Fiction," *American Literature,* XXVI (May, 1954), 141-153.

Gurney, Edmund, F. W. H. Myers, and Frank Podmore. *Phantasms of the Living*. London: Trubner, 1886.

Harnsberger, Caroline. *Mark Twain: Family Man*. New York: Citadel Press, 1960.

Howells, William Dean. *My Mark Twain: Reminiscences and Criticisms*. New York: Harper & Brothers, 1910.

James, William. *The Principles of Psychology*. 2 vols. New York: Henry Holt, 1890; reprinted by Dover Publications, 1950.

Jones, Alexander E. "Mark Twain and Freemasonry." *American Literature,* XXVI (November, 1954), 363-373.

————. "Mark Twain and the Determinism of *What Is Man?*" *American Literature,* XXIX (March, 1957), 1-17.

Laverty, Carroll D. "The Genesis of *The Mysterious Stranger*." *Mark Twain Quarterly,* VIII (Spring-Summer, 1947), 15-19.

Lawton, Mary. *A Lifetime with Mark Twain*. New York: Harcourt, Brace, 1925.

Leary, Lewis. *Mark Twain*. University of Minnesota Pamphlets on American Writers Series, No. 5. Minneapolis: University of Minnesota Press, 1960.

Lederer, Max. "Mark Twain in Vienna." *Mark Twain Quarterly,* VII (Summer-Fall, 1945), 1-12.

Long, E. Hudson. *Mark Twain Handbook*. New York: Hendricks, 1957.

"Lueger, Karl." *Encyclopædia Britannica*. Chicago: Britannica, Inc., 1950. Volume XIV.

"Mark Twain's Unedited and Unpublished Satire." *Current Opinion,* LXV (July, 1918), 48-49.

Lynn, Kenneth S. *Mark Twain and Southwestern Humor*. Boston: Little, Brown, 1959.

Paine, Albert Bigelow. *Mark Twain: A Biography*. 4 vols. New York: Gabriel Wells, 1923.

Parrington, Vernon Louis. *Main Currents in American Thought*. New York: Harcourt, Brace, 1927.

Parsons, Coleman O. "The Background of *The Mysterious Stranger.*" *American Literature,* XXXII (March, 1960) 55-74.

————. "The Devil and Samuel Clemens." *Virginia Quarterly Review,* XXIII (Autumn, 1947), 582-606.

Quick, Dorothy. *Enchantment: A Little Girl's Friendship with Mark Twain*. Norman: University of Oklahoma Press, 1961.

Salomon, Roger B. *Twain and the Image of History*. New Haven: Yale University Press, 1961.

Scott, Arthur L., ed. *Mark Twain: Selected Criticism*. Dallas: Southern Methodist University Press, 1955.

Schonemann, Friedrich. "Mark Twain and Adolf Wilbrandt." *Modern Language Notes,* XXXIV (June, 1919), 372-374.

Smith, Henry Nash. *Mark Twain: The Development of a Writer*. Cambridge, Mass.: Harvard University Press, 1962.

————. "Mark Twain's Image of Hannibal: From St. Petersburg to Eseldorf." *Texas Studies in English,* XXXVII (1958), 3-23.

Spiller, Robert E. *The Cycle of American Literature*. New York: Macmillan, 1955.

Stone, Albert E., Jr. *The Innocent Eye: Childhood in Mark Twain's Imagination*. New Haven: Yale University Press, 1961.

Twain, Mark. *Letters from the Earth,* ed. Bernard DeVoto. New York: Harper & Row, 1962.

————. *Mark Twain: Life as I Find It,* ed. Charles Neider. Garden City, New York: Hanover House, 1961.

————. *Mark Twain in Eruption,* ed. Bernard DeVoto. New York: Grosset & Dunlap, 1940.

————. *Mark Twain's Autobiography,* ed. Albert B. Paine. 2 vols. New York: Gabriel Wells, 1925.

————. *Mark Twain's Letters.* 2 vols. Arranged with comment by Albert Bigelow Paine. New York: Gabriel Wells, 1923.

————. *Mark Twain's Letters to Mary,* ed. Lewis Leary. New York: Columbia University Press, 1961.

————. *Mark Twain's Notebook,* ed. Albert Bigelow Paine. New York: Harper & Brothers, 1935.

————. *Report from Paradise,* ed. with introduction by Dixon Wecter. New York: Harper & Brothers, 1952.

————. *The Autobiography of Mark Twain,* ed. Charles Neider. New York: Harper & Brothers, 1959.

————. *The Love Letters of Mark Twain,* ed. Dixon Wecter. New York: Harper & Brothers, 1949.

————. *"The Mysterious Stranger" and Other Stories,* ed. Edmund Reiss. New York: New American Library of World Literature, 1962.

————. *The Portable Mark Twain,* ed. with introduction by Bernard DeVoto. New York: Viking Press, 1946.

————. *The Writings of Mark Twain.* 37 vols. New York: Gabriel Wells, 1922-1925.

Twain, Mark, and Howells, William D. *Mark Twain-Howells Letters: The Correspondence of Samuel L. Clemens and William D. Howells, 1872-1910,* ed. Henry Nash Smith and William M. Gibson with the assistance of Frederick Anderson. 2 vols. Cambridge, Mass.: Harvard University Press, 1960.

Wagenknecht, Edward. *Mark Twain: The Man and His Work.* Revised edition. Norman: University of Oklahoma Press, 1961.

Waggoner, Hyatt Howe. "Science in the Thought of Mark Twain," *American Literature,* VIII (January, 1937), 357-370.

Webster, Samuel C. *Mark Twain, Business Man.* Boston: Little, Brown, 1946.

Wecter, Dixon. "Mark Twain," in *Literary History of the United States.* Revised edition. New York: Macmillan, 1953, pp. 917-939.

————. *Sam Clemens of Hannibal.* Boston: Houghton Mifflin, 1952.

This book was set in Linotype Baskerville, a face known as a transitional design bridging the gap between "old style" and "modern style" faces. Text and covers were printed by C. E. Pauley and Co. of Indianapolis, the text on 60 lb. Warren's Old Style Antique stock, the covers on 65 lb. Tuscan cover stock. Cover engraving by Rheitone, Inc., Indianapolis. Cover design by Moroni St. John.

MARK TWAIN AND LITTLE SATAN reveals for the first time the story of Twain's creative work upon *The Mysterious Stranger*, the short novel that is the most important piece of fiction of his later years. He attempted at least three versions of this unusual tale of the supernatural. The chronology and circumstances of his composition of the several drafts have until now remained unknown—although the missing facts are a key to understanding what happened to Mark Twain and his work in his last years.

By his study of the original, unpublished manuscripts, the author has established the actual chronology of Twain's work upon them. His book charts the flow of the creative effort expended by Twain on his last great story during a period of eleven years.

MARK TWAIN AND LITTLE SATAN will make necessary and possible a major reappraisal and a new interpretation of the later life and writings of America's greatest author.

* * * * *

JOHN S. TUCKEY is associate professor of English at Purdue University's Calumet Campus. Born in Washington, D. C., he grew up in Indiana and received the B.A., M.A., and Ph.D. degrees at the University of Notre Dame. He has contributed articles to *Essays in Criticism* and *Journal of Developmental Reading*. He lives in Schererville, Indiana, with his wife, daughter, and son.

* * * * *

HENRY NASH SMITH, University of Califor[nia] [profes]sor and noted Twain scholar, says:

"Tuckey's conclusions about dates of composit[ion] several versions of *The Mysterious Stranger* differ from prevalent assumptions, but his marshaling internal and external evidence seems convincing opinion, his demonstration makes possible a fres[h] the investigation of Twain's later work . . . . Tucke[y's mono]graph will be indispensable to anyone seriously in the body of work that Bernard DeVoto called 'The Symbols of Despair.' "